Down the Rabbit Hole

Selma G. Lanes

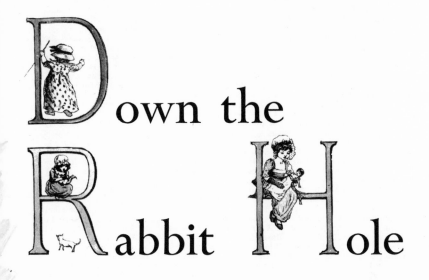

Down the
Rabbit Hole

Adventures & Misadventures in the
Realm of Children's Literature

Atheneum   1976   New York

The author gratefully acknowledges permission to reproduce illustrations from the following copyright works:
NO FIGHTING, NO BITING! by Else Holmelund Minarik. Illustration copyright © 1958 by Maurice Sendak. Reprinted by permission of Harper & Row, Publishers. / WHAT COLOR IS LOVE? by Joan Walsh Anglund. Copyright © 1966 by Joan Walsh Anglund. Reproduced by permission of Harcourt Brace Jovanovich, Inc. / CLEVER BILL by William Nicholson. Copyright © 1927 by William Nicholson. Reprinted by permission. / GET-A-WAY AND HÁRY JÁNOS by Maud and Miska Petersham. Copyright 1933 by Maud and Miska Petersham, copyright © renewed 1961 by Maud Petersham. Reprinted by permission of The Viking Press, Inc. / TIKKI TIKKI TEMBO retold by Arlene Mosel. Illustration copyright © 1968 by Blair Lent, Jr. Reproduced by permission of Holt, Rinehart and Winston, Inc. / ONE WIDE RIVER TO CROSS adapted by Barbara Emberley. Illustration copyright © 1966 by Ed Emberley. Reprinted by permission of Prentice-Hall, Inc. / MOMMY, BUY ME A CHINA DOLL adapted by Harve Zemach. Illustration copyright © 1966 by Margot Zemach. Reprinted by permission of Follett Publishing Company. / JOURNEYS OF SEBASTIAN by Fernando Krahn. Copyright © 1968 by Fernando Krahn and Dell Publishing Co., Inc. Reproduced by permission of Seymour Lawrence / Delacorte Press. / FREDERICK by Leo Lionni. Copyright © 1967 by Leo Lionni. Reprinted by permission of Pantheon Books, a division of Random House, Inc. / LITTLE BEAR by Else Holmelund Minarik. Illustration copyright © 1957 by Maurice Sendak. Reprinted with permission of Harper & Row, Publishers. / FATHER BEAR COMES HOME by Else Holmelund Minarik. Illustration copyright © 1959 by Maurice Sendak. Reprinted with permission of Harper & Row, Publishers. / THE LIGHT PRINCESS by George MacDonald. Illustration copyright © 1968 by Maurice Sendak. Reprinted with permission of Farrar, Straus & Giroux, Inc. / THE CAT IN THE HAT by Dr. Seuss. Copyright © 1957 by Theodor Seuss Geisel. Reprinted with permission of Random House, Inc. / THE BEST WORD BOOK EVER by Richard Scarry. Copyright © 1963 by Western Publishing Company, Inc. Reprinted by permission of Golden Press. / LITTLE HOUSE IN THE BIG WOODS by Laura Ingalls Wilder. Illustration copyright © 1953 by Garth Williams. Reprinted with permission of Harper & Row, Publishers. / TELL ME A MITZI by Lore Segal. Illustrations copyright © 1970 by Harriet Pincus. Reprinted with permission of Farrar, Straus & Giroux, Inc. / SOME OF THE DAYS OF EVERETT ANDERSON by Lucille Clifton. Illustration copyright © 1970 by Evaline Ness. Reproduced by permission of Holt, Rinehart and Winston, Inc. / THE LITTLE WOODEN FARMER by Alice Dalgliesh. Illustration copyright © 1968 by Anita Lobel. Reprinted with permission of The Macmillan Company. / THE LITTLE TRAIN by Lois Lenski. Copyright © 1940 by Lois Lenski. Reprinted with permission of Henry Z. Walck, Inc., Publishers. / THROW A KISS, HARRY by Mary Chalmers. Copyright © 1958 by Mary Chalmers. Reprinted with permission of Harper & Row, Publishers. / SLEEPY PEOPLE by M. B. Goffstein. Copyright © 1966 by M. B. Goffstein. Reprinted with permission of Farrar, Strauss, & Giroux, Inc. / ONE MONDAY MORNING by Uri Shulevitz. Copyright © 1967 by Uri Shulevitz. Reprinted with permission of Charles Scribner's Sons. / THE THREAD SOLDIER by Anne Heathers. Illustration copyright © 1960 by Esteban Frances. Reprinted with permission of Harcourt Brace Jovanovich, Inc. / THE WRONG SIDE OF THE BED by Edward Ardizzone. Copyright © 1970 by Edward Ardizzone. Reprinted with permission of Doubleday & Co., Inc. / THE HAT by Tomi Ungerer. Copyright © 1970 by Tomi Ungerer. Reprinted with permission of Parents' Magazine Press. / CHARLOTTE'S WEB by E. B. White. Illustration copyright © 1952 by Garth Williams. Reprinted with permission of Harper & Row, Publishers.

MAURICE SENDAK *No Fighting, No Biting!*

Acknowledgments

MY SPECIAL THANKS to Dick Kluger and Maurice Sendak for their enthusiasm, encouragement and moral support; to Estelle Miller and Edith Whiteman for a more concrete and earthbound support which had to do with remembering books and pictures, offering useful suggestions and cheerfully supplying references and sources from their own bookshelves at odd hours; to Judith and Shel Gordon, without whose help free time would have proved costly; to my mother and father and an understanding part-time employer who served occasionally as Ford Foundation surrogates with love and grace; to the late New York *Herald Tribune*'s *Book Week, Book World* and *The New York Times Book Review,* in whose pages many of the subjects of this book were first pursued; and to the publishers who have permitted me to reproduce illustrations from some notable children's books.

Introductory Note

WITH THE POSSIBLE EXCEPTION of advertising and the film, no popular art medium in our time has been as experimental, inventive and simply alive as children's books, particularly those for the younger age levels. Since the 1940s, a formidable array of first-rate talent has channeled itself into their creation: text, pictures and design. Sizable amounts of money are spent annually on their acquisition by schools, libraries, cultural enrichment programs and individual American parents; and healthy profits accrue to those publishers with strong lists of juvenile titles. Yet, nothing approaching the seriousness with which we take films—or, for that matter, advertisements—has yet been bestowed upon the consideration of young children's books. The focus of this work is on books for youngest listeners and readers, viewed not as passing amusements scarcely meriting a grownup's serious attention but, at their best, as legitimate contributions to the larger world of literature.

The three media—advertising, the film and young children's books—have much in common. First, there is an immense technical virtuosity, of machinery and men, at the disposal of the large number of practitioners in each field. Second, the efficiency of this production machinery itself tends to encourage further production independent of either the content of what is being produced or a recognition of the saturation point of their respective publics for even superior offerings. As for films, since the close of World War II, audiences have been getting and demanding more and more of the art of cinema, as can be witnessed both by the great number of innovative films produced in the '50s and '60s and by the proliferation of serious criticism of the medium. Advertising, too, in the same period has come of age. Not only has the field developed increasing numbers of sophisticated copywriters, account executives and talented artists (a surprising number of whom eventually defect to the field of children's picture books), but the public itself has grown more sophisticated and demanding. Saturated by advertising via newspaper, magazine, radio and TV, it will sit up and take note of only the best of that medium's blandishments. In children's books, however, Corinthians I (13:1) still provides the likeliest key to our critical neutrality and distance: "When I was a child, I spake as a child . . . when I became a man I put away childish things." How the cow jumped over the moon, after all, is surely not a legitimate subject for mature conjecture.

The literature of childhood is thus herded into safe enclosures where, unfortunately, judgment is often scaled down to pint size and standards of excellence are indulgently slackened. The major weekly book-review supplements acknowledge the genre with a page of cheerful potpourri plot scannings. Twice yearly, entire Sunday supplements are devoted to juvenile books, a beneficence prompted more by the numbers of titles now being produced and advertised each season than by the degree of seriousness with which the genre is regarded. While there is one magazine of repute devoted in its entirety to children's books and their authors, surely its genteel prose and self-congratulatory tone often smack more of class notes in an alumni quarterly than the astringent and measured judgments that characterize critical writing in such periodicals as *Partisan Review, The New York Review of Books* and *Film Quarterly.*

This is not to suggest that what the field of children's books most lacks today is either longer or weightier reviewing. One may even suspect that Graham Greene had at least the tip of his tongue in cheek when, in a perceptive essay on Beatrix Potter some years ago, he referred to *Peter Rabbit* as "the second of the great comedies" (the first being *The Tale of Two Bad Mice*). Surely small children's books cannot easily bear such weighty literary mantles. It is, in fact, entirely possible that whole categories of worthwhile books for young children are a-verbal in nature and are best judged by some sensitive non-word yardstick. Like coin of the realm, they simply ring true in the attentive listener's ear. It is a major purpose of this book to seek out and perhaps isolate the units of measurement that distinguish the true literature of early childhood from the quantities of dross annually published.

But how do we begin to look at, or listen attentively to, young children's books? What of those voices that, grown to adult register, still elect to speak to children? Have they settled for a second-best audience? Or are there sensibilities that speak not sweet nothings but such truths as put the children and adults who read them in closer touch with their inner selves? Are there such things as constant childish tastes down through the generations and authentic voices of childhood? Or are children's books merely a subtle and evanescent form of propaganda through which we feed each generation's offspring sugar-coated doses of current adult beliefs, hopes and concerns? And, pertinent to the focus of this work, how can we explain the unprecedented popularity of the picture book in our time? Is it, as Marshall McLuhan would have us believe, a harbinger of that "new world of accelerated transcience . . . the picture-gestalt culture," or has it, rather, more to do with the changing nature of childhood itself?

Less than a century ago, the United States was a quite different country, greatly underpopulated, overrich in opportunity for the adventurous, and with grownup inhabitants who looked upon their offspring as raw material to be molded and tempered into responsible and productive adults—the sooner the better. Since death rates were higher and tasks abundant for any able hands, new grownups were in constant demand. But today, in this country and in most technologically advanced cultures, finding a productive use for increasing numbers of healthy, often highly skilled adults already in the population is a real problem. Thus, childhood has become, more and more, a state to be savored fully and preserved as long as possible. This has done much to alter the focus of, and market for, young children's books. There are books today for children scarcely able to sit up in their cribs; yet reading matter for those eight and up is considerably less oriented toward adult life than most of the stories the magazine *St. Nicholas* offered its young American readers, aged six to eighteen, in the last decades of the nineteenth century. While many books in the eight-to-twelve age group have in recent years grown bolder in their willingness to tackle controversial subject matter—sex, drugs, theft, alienation —the point of view is generally a peer-group one with little to interest a wider audience.

A century and even less ago, the printed word seemed better able to bridge generations. Other diversions being fewer, individuals of all ages depended more on one another for entertainment. Reading aloud within families and among neighbors was a popular pastime. Grandmothers, grandfathers, aunts and uncles often lived nearby to enrich children's lives with their own stories. There was a more natural rapport among persons of all ages. Today, young families more often than not live at great distance from all near relations, and books have become, in part, a substitute for that close human contact children once had with a number of their elders. Where grownups formerly spent long hours in children's company—while baking their own bread, chopping firewood, milking cows, sewing and washing clothes by hand—simply because they lived in a simpler, slower-moving age, today both parents may be working away from the home and many young children are bundled off to nursery school by the age of three. Perhaps one reason why the seemingly unending parade of fairy-tale adaptations, ABCs and first books of animals, nursery rhymes, learning to tie shoes and tell time, etc., all seem to find buyers is that they are filling a real and deep *companionship* void. That leisurely one-to-one relationship between parent and child, neighbor and child or grandparent and child is becoming rarer or, in any case, briefer. The growing isolation of the young from those elders who, in other times, would have taught them a wide variety of life's basic lessons has put an increasing burden on children's books to fill the gap. This new distance between the daily lives of adults and children is assuredly a factor encouraging the proliferation of books for the very young.

Almost all existing studies and surveys of children's literature have been chronological and historical, giving substance and literary respectability to a slighted genre by cataloging and characterizing its varied fare. One notable exception is Eleanor Cameron's *The Green and Burning Tree,* which explores as no other book ever has the sources of artistic inspiration and literary merits of books for reading children. The chapters that follow are frankly idiosyncratic, based on predilection after much reading to my own children and for myself in the course of reviewing and writing books for young children. With no claims to professional expertise, I hope that out of a kind of introspection not usually lavished on young children's books as literature there will emerge certain rock-like verities and hallmarks that may enable interested parents and admirers of the genre to take not only children's books but some of the subtler aspects of childhood itself more seriously. It is time attentive ears and eyes began to make value judgments concerning the worth and direction of our children's books. There is no question that too many books, and too few of these of lasting—or even lingering—merit, are produced each year, often by superior illustrators and with the encouragement of the most reputable publishing houses. It is time sights were trained on what Walter de la Mare deemed the young deserved—''only the rarest kind of best.''

S.G.L

Contents

Illustrations

xii

Illustrations

The illuminated initials on the title page and at the beginning of each chapter are reproduced from *Kate Greenaway's Alphabet*.

"I know well that only the rarest kind of best in anything can be good enough for the young."

Walter de la Mare

". . . he who pleases children will be remembered with pleasure by men."

James Boswell

1: Children, Grownups and Literature

*Infancy is what is eternal, and the rest, all the
rest is brevity, extreme brevity.*

ANTONIO PORCHIA

HE REGRET we have for our childhood is not wholly
justifiable,'' Robert Louis Stevenson once wrote in a
perceptive essay called ''Child's Play.'' Then, proceeding to list a few of the non-regrets, he noted,
''Terror is gone out of our lives, moreover; we no
longer see the devil in the bed curtains nor lie awake to listen to
the wind . . . we are set free forever from the daily fear of
chastisement.''

This somewhat dour if wholly realistic view of one side of
childhood is hardly the one that most adults have in mind when
making choices of what constitutes good and appropriate reading
matter for children. More in keeping with the attitude of the
grownup browser through bookstore or library shelf is Wordsworth's rosier ''Heaven lies about us in our infancy,'' and it is
this often unacknowledged longing on the part of adults for celes-
tial fare for small children which imposes on their books a burden
that only the best authors and illustrators manage to overcome.
This burden is inescapable, for children's books, unlike any other

3

literature, are always first judged by those outside their intended audience. To start with, they are written and published by grownups; secondly, they are most often bought by other grownups for children. Thirdly, children are notoriously unreliable critics, as J. R. R. Tolkien has pointed out: "They like or try to like what is given to them; if they do not like it, they cannot well express their dislike or give reasons for it. . . ." Thus, those children's books which endure do so because a generation of children grown to adulthood still remembers them with pleasure (some small part of which is certainly nostalgia) and introduces them to their own children. The process is unlikely ever to undergo much change.

Future children will doubtless have no greater success or interest in writing books for their peers than those of the past. A quick rereading of *The Young Visiters,* that precocious Victorian confection by the eight-year-old Daisy Ashford, reveals that no promising solutions lie here. Mr. Salteena's and Ethel's adventures are hilarious to adults for the glimpses they afford of one child's world view and of her shrewd observation of grownup pretensions:

> These compartments are the haunts of the Aristockracy said
> the earl and they are kept going by people who have got
> something funny in their family and who want to be less mere
> if you can comprehend.

Miss Ashford's abiding passion for "carriages full of costly people" and clean underclothing, while genuinely funny and childlike, did not produce a book that many children have ever taken to their hearts. The truth of the matter is that the seeming simplicity and innocence we as adults prize in children's books

4

seldom arise from either innocence or simplicity but rather—as in all true literature—from a deep experience of the world intelligently digested and sensitively transformed. It was Stevenson again who remarked that however much we may admire the best of writers for their breadth of range, their grasp of nuance and life's complexity, in the end we must always acknowledge "that simplification was their method, and simplicity their excellence." Yet those authors we enjoy most, whether writing for adult or child, do not present a simple world, but rather, through artful simplification and with clear-eyed vision, light some aspects of an infinitely complicated one. There should be, then, no difference *qualitatively* in the criteria by which we judge young children's and adults' literature. Yet, an instinctive tendency to idealize early childhood (if not individual children) usually creeps in to obscure this fact.

This regressive force at play when most of us view children's books is what might be called the "Peter Pan Principle." We are reluctant to ruffle that blanket of primal innocence with which all children enter the world. (The late Paul Hazard, the French scholar and romantic, was a champion of this viewpoint of "childhood as a fortunate island where happiness must be protected.") The result has often been books so sunshine-saturated and corruption-free as to be antiseptic, devoid of any living substance. "The process of growing older," Tolkien has observed, "is not necessarily allied to growing wickeder, though the two do often happen together." Most of us, however, would share the opinion of the seventeenth-century English philosopher John Earle that "the elder he [a child] grows, he is a stair lower from God," and we are, all of us, reluctant in any way to hasten the descent. (The contemporary author Maia Wojciechowska wrote in a *New York Times* review of a collection of children's prose in 1969: "It makes clear what I knew all along: the younger the child the more beautiful his thought process, for growth of the body tends to constrict the workings of the mind.")

To be an adult, then, is to view childhood at a great distance, through the wide end of the telescope, and possibly to invest the state with idealized abstractions. This remains true despite the psychological sophistication of our century and the close attention that has been given to behavioral science and developmental studies of children. (Certainly children view adults across an even wider gulf. Who of us failed to grow up in the firm belief that we occupied the dead center of our parents' every waking thought? It is only the child arrived at parenthood who realizes, for the first time, how many other concerns share that center with children, occasionally even nudging them well outside its periphery.) For grownups, this remote and essentially literary attitude toward childhood usually begins with the birth of a particular child. To each parent, relative or interested bystander within the orbit of any given infant, its birth heralds an exhilarating sense of the world's renewal, of hope reborn.

> A child more than all other gifts
> That earth can offer to declining man
> Brings hope with it, and forward-looking thoughts,

wrote William Wordsworth, and George Eliot gave the sentiment a resounding seconding by taking it as the opening note of her *Silas Marner*. A new baby is a slate unmarked, yet another possibility to achieve that perfection we adults well know we have fallen short of; a new chance to avoid and correct mistakes made by parents, grandparents and their parents before them.

For a brief period of time after the birth of a child, a piece of the world's future seems to rest wholly and portentously in our hands. When, therefore, a grown person chooses a book for a young child, the act is often freighted with odd bits of this heavy if nebulous luggage: the unspoken responsibility not to sully that living possibility for perfection reborn with each new being. The weight of our future hopes, as well as our past regrets, is the invisible burden that young children's books always bear.

On the other hand, to be a parent or any grownup in the real world who works at close range with children is to be constantly made aware of one's shortcomings in dealing with these flesh-and-blood possibilities for perfection. In how many trying situations are we shocked to find ourselves responding exactly as an erring mother or insensitive teacher once did to us, rather than as those reasoning, all-wise Olympians we had hoped (in solitary musings) we could be and our children (in innocence and dependency) often erroneously assume we are. One of the little-acknowledged joys of young children's books is that they allow us, adult and child, momentarily to escape from failures and inadequacies, from spilled milk and overharsh scoldings, into a more tranquil world where any problem posed generally has a satisfactory answer. It was Kenneth Grahame who divulged the secret that grownups, as well as children, seek "relief" in the world of children's literature. There can be no doubt that we all find in books for the very young a world both simpler and better ordered than the one we customarily inhabit. The elemental questions raised in a picture book or more elaborate tale will be comfortingly resolved before the last page is turned, and no matter how black a given day has been for grownup or child, something has turned out right if it closes with a good bedtime story.

At one and the same time that adults romanticize the state of childhood (and are often brought harshly back to reality by individual children), there is a part of each of us which is as close to the book being read as the four-year-old who solemnly listens. There is remarkably little difference between a child's and an adult's response to Kipling's *The Elephant's Child,* or to Oscar Wilde's *The Happy Prince,* or to L. Frank Baum's cheerfully absurd *The Magical Monarch of Mo.* (This can be easily verified by anyone who attends a Punch-and-Judy show with children. The faces of adult and child register much the same mixed delight and horror.) "What is an adult?" Simone de Beauvoir asks rhetorically in *The Woman Destroyed.* "A child puffed with age." We do not shed our childhoods. Somewhere, often not far beneath those layers of experience and education we have assimilated, is that child who faced the world new and untried a generation or more ago.

The children's books that touch us most deeply are those which somehow manage to reach this basic, childlike core. Perhaps to savor truly the best of children's literature, or to take it as seriously as it deserves, we must first possess some inventory of what remains to us of our own childhoods. "I know," wrote Walter de la Mare,

> that in later life it is just . . . possible now and again to recover fleetingly the intense delight, the untellable joy and happiness and fear and grief and pain of our early years, of an all but forgotten childhood. I have, in a flash, in a momentary glimpse, seen again a horse, an oak, a daisy, just as I saw them in those early years, as if with that heart, with those senses.

And surely Marcel Proust's *Swann's Way*, in which the author-narrator re-creates the emotional climate of his childhood in Paris and at Combray, constitutes the most complete inventory in adult literature of childhood's legacy to the individual:

> My sole consolation when I went upstairs for the night was that Mamma would come in and kiss me after I was in bed. But this good night lasted for so short a time: she went down again so soon that the moment in which I heard her climb the stairs, and then caught the sound of her garden dress of blue muslin, from which hung little tassels of plaited straw, rustling along the double-doored corridor, was for me a moment of the keenest sorrow. So much did I love that good night that I reached the stage of hoping that it would come as late as possible, so as to prolong the time of respite during which Mamma would not yet have appeared. . . .

From my own childhood I occasionally recapture, when nursing a cold, the soothing taste of mashed potatoes with butter eaten long ago after severe bouts of sore throat. And on certain bright April days I can feel again the liberating caress of a spring breeze on bare knees just as it felt each year on that marvelous, miraculous day when my mother let me abandon my heavy winter lisle stockings for the first time. That free, lighter-than-air sensation between knee socks and skirt will forever mean spring to me.

But is this sort of thing all? No, there are also remembered terrors and fears. Shapeless, unreasoned, they were wholly compelling and largely secret from any adults round about. In my own bedroom as a child there was a big, dark walk-in closet where once, at the age of five or six, I hid the sad remains of a beloved wooden Felix the Cat toy. The cat, about eighteen inches long, its arms and legs made of painted outsize wooden beads strung ingeniously on elastic bands, was a gift my parents had brought home from a trip. Felix was so pliable that he could hold a salute or assume sitting, running, standing or acrobatic positions. While being put briskly through his paces one morning, Felix snapped and crumbled into a pathetic heap of meaningless beads. Though I was surely upset by his unexpected demise— why else the persistence of the memory?—my grief had barely surfaced before I felt compelled to secrete Felix's remains in a black corner at the very back of this dark closet. I was desperately afraid of what my mother would say if she discovered that he was broken. I had not the slightest doubt that the accident was all my fault or that my mother would react like the Old Testament God of Wrath. Though death could not have wrenched him more suddenly or irrevocably from the orbit of my treasured possessions, I refused to acknowledge his absence either then or even after his discovery. When my mother finally came on the sad, abandoned bead cluster, perhaps a week after his unceremonious interment, I said with feigned indifference (but what I knew in the depths of my being to be the supreme betrayal of a loved friend), "Oh, is he broken?" To the world, my grief was effectively disguised and my burden of anxiety and guilt invisible. Even a part of myself was taken in by the ruse.

Once fully grown, we tend to forget, or at least to undervalue this sort of real and secret suffering all children undergo. As Maurice Sendak has noted, "The realities of childhood put to shame the half-true notions in some children's books." Busily coping with pressing problems of "real life" as we see it now, we forget that children too have a highly developed sense of their own lives and dignity, the importance of their games, toys and fantasies. It is a dignity all too easily violated by adult anger, indifference or laughter. The children we all were and those we buy books for today bear some resemblance to icebergs. A major part of their affective lives—where they are really at— lies hidden from adult view and understanding. In children, as in grownups, it is this part which literature principally addresses.

Those voices we most enjoy in young children's books are the ones which somehow manage to straddle the years and tap this subterranean core in us all. There is Frank Stockton, who tells us of a fine old king in *Ting-a-Ling Tales:*

> His queen being dead, his whole affection was given to his only child, The Princess Aufalia; and, whenever he happened to think of it, he paid great attention to her education. She had the best of masters of embroidery and in the language of flowers, and took lessons on the zither three times a week.

What resonance "whenever he happened to think of it" has in adult ears! Beatrix Potter manages the same embrace of the generations with her chaste and supple prose. When Miss Potter writes of rabbits, there is none of that soft, cuddly, nose-twitching frippery about them. Her abiding and almost clinical interest in small animals predated her thinking about writing books for children. "Benjamin once fell into an aquarium head first," she writes of a pet rabbit in an entry in her journal, "and sat in the water which he could not get out of, pretending to eat a piece of string. Nothing like putting a face upon circumstances." In another entry, she noted: "Rabbits are creatures of warm, volatile temperament but shallow and absurdly transparent." It is this

11

clear-eyed vision that informs her best tales and lifts them above trivia to true literature. What we respond to in the work of the best authors and illustrators for children is the honesty and wholeheartedness of the experiences they render. Kate Greenaway was herself wholly entranced by English rural life and the rustic comfort and simplicity she found in the country houses of relatives she visited as a child. It is this adult nostalgia for pre-industrial England which raises her work from mere quaint and ornamental costuming to documents of historical authenticity. What we respond to in the best illustrations of Arthur Rackham—his carefully rendered fabrics, his lovingly reproduced crockery, slippers and old dressing gowns—is the robustness of reality conveyed. The adults who write and illustrate best for children are never those solicitous of preserving innocence in their readers but are rather those charmed beings who somehow manage to preserve in themselves an innocence and purity of response to whatever experiences they encounter. We delight in the child-like quality of their enthusiasms rather than in a subject matter that has been tailor-made for children's consumption.

The fact of the matter is there is no subject matter specially suited to children. Surely all children see and feel much more than most adults care, or perhaps dare, to give them credit for experiencing. When my younger son was two years old, we had living a floor above us in a small New York apartment house a ninety-year-old woman, frail, crooked and cheerful. We often met her in the elevator, as her chief outdoor activity was walking a fat and aged dog several times a day. Since she genuinely liked small children, having been a governess for many years in her youth, our encounters were always pleasant. As winter came, however, she was more and more housebound, one ailment following on another. The few times we met now she had grown visibly more bent and birdlike, almost transparent in her fragility. Instead of seeing us in the elevator, she often peered down from over the fifth-floor landing when we emerged from our apartment. She would stand there silently and somehow longingly as if we, healthy and mobile, existed on a different level of being. She was merely an invisible spectator from some no-man's-land. Because she was so small and frail and the hall light none too good, there was often no way of knowing she was there unless she coughed or one of us happened to peer up into the shadows. Once my son had noticed her, however, and knew she was likely to be there, he clutched my hand fearfully and clung to my skirt whenever we left our apartment. Though she had been his good friend only a few months before, it was as if he now sensed a threat in her presence—of the unknown, of death perhaps, or merely of the inexplicable transformation that had taken place to turn his friend into this specter of human powerlessness floating above us. He has, by now, probably forgotten the actual experience, but somewhere in his mind—as in the minds of all children, I am sure—there remains such a semi-invisible figure capable of being roused, even explained and made less dark and fearsome, by literature.

The one unassailable statement that can be made about everyone's childhood is that it is fleeting. Once past, we remember little of our own and possibly less of our children's. The triumph of first steps—that stately if tottery march of infants, so miraculous to each and every parent seeing it—is quickly superseded by the mastery of a flight of stairs, first phrases uttered, the pedaling of a tricycle. Childhood's victories are building blocks, stacked one upon the other before there is time to memorialize a given one.

As children, we are far too involved in the challenges of daily growth and accomplishments to remember much of yesterday's triumphs. And, as parents, we are too busy keeping up with the laundry, daily airings, bills, baths and getting the supper to remember more than a few of the highest and lowest points. Pictures we lovingly save to frame on our children's walls become too infantile before we get around to mounting them. And I can remember the genuine pain I felt on seeing a small boy—perhaps three—in a blue sailor suit from out of a bus window one morning, when I realized that both of my own sons were already beyond the age for such outfits. I had forgotten this classic garb of boyhood, and now they would never wear sailor suits in my later memories of them.

Furthermore, the state of childhood is self-consuming, devouring even those material appurtenances we might remember it by. Favorite toys are broken and lost; clothing is outgrown; books are torn and discarded. I know an otherwise sensible and unsentimental mother who preserved the remains of her second child's umbilical cord in a ceramic dish in her kitchen cabinet. She intended to paste it in a memory book to present to him when he was fully grown. It would represent certain proof that he had been an infant, to herself possibly as well as to him.

Were children's books good for little else, then, they give both adults and children pause, a time to contemplate and catch hold of some ephemeral moment, to feel its weight and savor its substance. Particularly at the youngest age level, children's books are often much like snapshots. They record the child's triumphs: making a friend, mastering a skill (counting, saying the ABCs, identifying animals). And thus they put him in touch with himself by underscoring those experiences he may not have noticed in the course of living them. If we cannot remember what it was like to be three, we can remember the pleasure and suspense of hearing *Peter Rabbit* for the first, or even the hundredth, time.

"In one's mature years," Howard Pyle wrote, "one forgets the books that one reads, but the stories of childhood leave an indelible impression, and their author always has a niche in the temple of memory from which the image is never cast out to be thrown into the rubbish-heap of things that are outgrown and outlived."

MAY, 1876.

St. Nicholas

SCRIBNER'S
Illustrated Magazine
FOR
GIRLS and BOYS

CONDUCTED BY

MARY MAPES DODGE

Vol. III.   No. 7.

SCRIBNER & CO.
NEW YORK.

FRED'K WARNE & CO. Bedford St. Strand, LONDON.

2: *Who Killed* St. Nicholas?

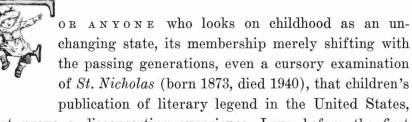OR ANYONE who looks on childhood as an unchanging state, its membership merely shifting with the passing generations, even a cursory examination of *St. Nicholas* (born 1873, died 1940), that children's publication of literary legend in the United States, must prove a disconcerting experience. Long before the first publishing house in this country launched the first American juvenile department—Macmillan in 1919—the strong, patrician voice of *St. Nicholas* had made itself heard across the land on behalf of the children of the brave New World. And those children, literate, earnest, often isolated and starved for intelligent diversion and communication with the wide world beyond their doorsteps, bore only a fleeting resemblance to the children for whom books are written today. In its way, *St. Nicholas* did as much to open up the unexplored hinterland of literature for them as the railroads did to open up the vast expanses of the West to their parents and grandparents.

The magazine had its beginnings in July of 1873 when a

succinct article on "Editing for the Young," unsigned, appeared in *Scribner's Magazine.* Its author, obviously familiar with the some threescore magazines and Sunday-school papers produced for children in this country in the immediate post–Civil War era, wrote: "We edit for the approval of fathers and mothers and endeavor to make the child's monthly a milk-and-water variety of the adult's periodical. But, in fact, the child's magazine needs to be stronger, truer, bolder, more uncompromising than the other. Its cheer must be the cheer of the bird song, not of condescending editorial babble . . . no sermonizing either, no wearisome spinning out of facts, nor rattling of the dry bones of history . . . the ideal child's magazine is a pleasure ground." The article's appearance in *Scribner's* at this moment was hardly fortuitous, since its anonymous author, Mary Mapes Dodge, had just been engaged by *Scribner's* itself to plan and produce a new children's magazine of quality. Few persons have ever seen in clearer perspective the limited but vital role literature can play in children's lives. "What delights us in Milton, Keats and Tennyson," she wrote in the same piece, "children often find for themselves in stars, daisies and such joys and troubles as little ones know. . . . Literary skill in its highest is but the subtle thinning of the veil that life and time have thickened."

Mrs. Dodge, herself the author in 1865 of the world's first international best-selling juvenile novel, *Hans Brinker, or the Silver Skates,* was not inexperienced as an editor. She had helped her father, James Mapes, to put out a progressive magazine on agriculture called *The Working Farmer* and, more recently, had served as household editor of a leading women's magazine of the time, *Hearth and Home.* Her ideas on illustration for children were definite as well. "Pictures," she wrote, "should be heartily conceived and well-executed. . . . If it be only the picture of a cat, it must be so like a cat that it will do its own purring and not sit a dead, stuffed thing, requiring the editor to purr for it.'' As for the editor of the child's magazine, she insisted, in an era when permissiveness was as yet unheard of regarding the attitude adults maintained toward their young, that ''he must give just what the child demands, and to do this successfully is a matter of instinct, without which no man should presume to be a child's editor and go unhung.'' In the same issue of *Scribner's* her bold and forthright pronouncements were immediately followed by an article titled ''Recollections of a Restored Lunatic,'' which may or may not have been an expression of some other editor's skepticism.

In November of that year, *St. Nicholas: Scribner's Illustrated Magazine for Girls and Boys Conducted by Mary Mapes Dodge*—its full baptismal name—first appeared; and few who knew it then or since have disputed that it quickly became and for some fifty years remained the high-water mark of quality in American children's literature. For thirty-two years Mrs. Dodge herself personally ''conducted'' this child's symphony of a magazine, cajoling work from such writers as Frank Stockton, Frances Hodgson Burnett, L. Frank Baum, Sarah Orne Jewett, Sidney Lanier, Bret Harte, Joel Chandler Harris and William Cullen Bryant. (For every name one mentions, another as well known could take its place.) *St. Nicholas* not only published the best writers of its time, but encouraged its own young readers to contribute (at first only letters, but later original artwork and text), competing for the magazine's gold and silver badges of merit. Among its distinguished child contributors were Henry Luce, Edna St. Vincent Millay, Rachel Field, Ring Lardner, Stephen

Vincent Benét, Robert Benchley, Eudora Welty, Cornelia Otis Skinner and E. B. White. Hardly a well-known author of the time was absent from *St. Nicholas'* pages, and many a literary figure of the 1920s and '30s began his life in print in *St. Nicholas.* The very completeness of Mrs. Dodge's list of contributors attests both to the quality of her contents and to the high degree of literacy in her readership. The magazine so quickly outranked all its competitors that by the mid-'80s, the struggling young illustrator Howard Pyle could write home to his mother, "There is no other child's magazine of any worth in the country."

When Mrs. Dodge met the much lionized Rudyard Kipling at a New York dinner party in the 1890s, the author, already world-famous for his poetry and adult writings, expressed a desire to write something for *St. Nicholas.* The magazine's success and patrician standards were so well established by this time that Mrs. Dodge could ask, only partly in jest, "Are you sure you are equal to it?" The Mowgli stories, later to become *The Jungle Book* and *The Second Jungle Book,* were first published in *St. Nicholas,* as were the *Just So Stories,* Kipling's wholehearted response to her challenge.

Praising *St. Nicholas* toward the end of its fruitful life, Alice M. Jordan, children's librarian at Boston's Public Library, wrote in 1930, "No periodical for children was ever started under happier auspices than *St. Nicholas* and none has contributed so largely in establishing high standards for children's books." For anyone interested in American children's literature or the quality of childhood then and now, the magazine provides an unparalleled sourcebook. So much that Mrs. Dodge was able to take for granted in her time has vanished from our own that the simple recognition of the changes goes a long way toward defining the character of children's book publishing today.

There was, to begin with, the very name *St. Nicholas*. Mrs. Dodge conceived of it while riding in a horse-drawn cab up Broadway to her 57th Street apartment one evening following a late editorial meeting. What could be more appropriate, she decided, than "the boys' and girls' own Saint," who, as it happened, was also the patron saint of the old Dutch city which was to be the magazine's cosmopolitan home? ("Another thing you know," Mrs. Dodge confided to her readers in the inaugural issue, revealing her sensitivity to children's standards of judgment: "He is fair and square. He comes when he says he will.") In the year 1873 there was no question of the predominant character of the nation's population. A Protestant, Anglo-Saxon hegemony existed and was accepted as a matter of course. The contents of *St. Nicholas* were heavily weighted with fiction and non-fiction about English and Scottish history. An account of Charles Dickens' early life with his family in the Marshalsea Prison for debtors identified the author as "the beloved novelist of the Anglo-Saxon people," with no doubt that the American reader was part of that group. *St. Nicholas* was, as John Greenleaf Whittier wrote in another context for the magazine,

> Marvelous to our tough old stock
> Chips o' the Anglo-Saxon block.

The very names of so many of its authors—all tripartite— are evidence of the pride of largely English origin: Albert Bigelow Paine, Laura Ingalls Wilder, Helen Hunt Jackson, Thomas Bailey Aldrich, Kate Douglas Wiggin, Edward Everett Hale, William Dean Howells, Richard Harding Davis.

Mrs. Dodge herself came of such old American stock. Her

father, left a comfortable fortune from a family cloth-importing business, was able to indulge his gentlemanly interests both in agricultural theory and in journalism. Frequent visitors at the Mapes house at 32 Greenwich Street in New York included Horace Greeley, editor of the *Tribune,* and the poet William Cullen Bryant. The household was highly literate, with a distinct moral tone, as were most of the households into which *St. Nicholas* monthly came. In our day, the latter-day offspring of generations of emigration from other parts of Europe and elsewhere are automatically part of "the pluralistic society" (the product of "the melting pot" that the United States became in *St. Nicholas'* mid-career). No nationally circulated magazine today could dream of taking so parochial and obviously Christian a name as *St. Nicholas.*

Mrs. Dodge's nine-point credo for *St. Nicholas,* as set forth in the first issue, is also highly revealing of its archaisms in the context of the present day. *St. Nicholas'* gallant aims were:

1. To give clean, genuine fun to children of all ages.
2. To give them examples of the finest types of boyhood and girlhood.
3. To inspire them with an appreciation of fine pictorial art.
4. To cultivate the imagination in profitable directions.
5. To foster a love of country, home, nature, truth, beauty and sincerity.
6. To prepare boys and girls for life as it is.
7. To stimulate their ambitions—but along normally progressive lines.
8. To keep pace with a fast-moving world in all its activities.

9. To give reading matter which every parent may pass to his children unhesitatingly.

When *St. Nicholas* spoke of "children of all ages," it really meant children aged six to seventeen, a span no publisher of book or magazine for children would dream of attempting today. Just as our increasingly complex society has done away with such occupations as tinker (replaced by specialists like the licensed color-TV repairman) and family doctor (superseded by the more august and learned internist), so too childhood has become a series of compartmentalized periods of specialized growth. Youngest children are the ages-two-to-four category for purposes of selecting their literary entertainment. If they are precocious, the bookseller will proffer something from the three-to-six-year-old literary garden plot; but, from infancy through mid-teenage, children's books are seldom sold or reviewed except within narrow and often meaningless age groupings. *St. Nicholas* is almost incomprehensible in an era when a magazine called *Seventeen* has found an audience—1,400,000 monthly—bigger than Mrs. Dodge's entire readership (100,000 monthly) during the years her magazine was the country's most popular juvenile publication.

Not only were children in Mrs. Dodge's day fewer but the nature of their childhood was entirely different from that of to-day's progeny. The United States, if beyond its roughest pioneering days, was still in its late homesteading phase, and most families outside the few big cities lived isolated, self-sufficient lives. Children were not only depended upon as contributing members of their families at a much earlier age, but children of all ages within a family were dependent upon one another for companionship, recreation and often even education. The one-room schoolhouse was in its heyday and no child was oriented toward his peer group. It was entirely likely that the nearest child one's own age lived five or ten miles off. That sort of beautiful 1960s picture book aimed at the two-to-four-year-old set, following the flight of a butterfly from flower to flower in four delectable colors and using a vocabulary of only a dozen familiar words, would probably have had no takers—assuming it could have been produced—for the book buyer then looked for something with broader range and more long-term sustenance for the entire family's long evenings at home.

This *St. Nicholas* provided in abundance. There were Frank Stockton's antic fairy tales; Louisa May Alcott's "spinning wheel stories" of earlier times in the American wilderness; Theodore Roosevelt on buffalo hunting; stories of the crossing of the *Mayflower* and the settling of the colonies; sagas of frontier life, of runaway trains, of plantation living, adventure tales of the sea and the story of Stanley's trek through Africa told by a member of his expedition. In a day when newspapers often reached the countryside only after the news was disappointingly stale and other reading matter was scarce, whole families joined happily to hear the latest Lucretia P. Hale installment of *The Peterkin Papers,* to read a highly literate account of the life of Beethoven (or perhaps Washington Irving) by Ariadne Gilbert, or even accept a delightful and urbane lesson on "How to Study Pictures" from Charles H. Caffin. After all, no well-endowed big-city museum was just around the corner, and culture, far from being scorned or taken for granted, had the increased value of all scarce commodities.

In the '80s and '90s, all of literate America could be viewed as one large family. One's grandmother's grandmother was probably witness to events leading to the nation's founding. (In fact, one *St. Nicholas* author wrote of just such a great-great-grandmother.) The magazine's readership sprang, almost without exception, from the same sort of hard-working, forward-looking American stock. The cheerful optimism of writers and readers alike was based on the solid achievements of the new nation their own families had successfully carved out of an abundant wilderness. Their common heritage gave them a common outlook on the world, and the subject matter of *St. Nicholas* seldom strained for relevance to the lives of its readers. It was born of the readership's common American experience, a healthy communality almost totally lost today to children's literature.

Among the great strengths of *St. Nicholas* was its unshakable belief that a function of children's literature was to impart "examples of the finest types of boyhood and girlhood," that it could and should "foster a love of country, home, nature, truth, beauty and sincerity." Theodore Roosevelt could write during his Presidency a piece entitled "What We May Expect of the American Boy" and say, "In life, as in a football game, the principles to follow are: 'Don't foul, don't flinch, hit the line hard'" with no danger of being considered a stuffed shirt or an old windbag. No one among editors or readers doubted for a moment that life was full of rich rewards or that the business of every American child was to grow up to be a productive, hard-working American adult. There was no crisis of values, for neither adults nor children had yet lost the faith that America could and would ultimately reach perfection. That certitude, of course, has long since disappeared from more than children's literature. Our present-day children's books are more likely to be beautiful, clever and tasteful—marvels of production know-how, bearers of instant aesthetic pleasure— but with little deliberate effort to impart values. Walter D. Edmonds, who has written of earlier times and won a Newbery Award for his suspense-filled *The Matchlock Gun,* has spoken of this marked change: "There seems to me to be a definite tendency everywhere to keep our children children as long as we can, instead of pointing to man's and woman's estate as the great aim of their lives." This duty *St. Nicholas* never shirked.

When in 1874 something akin to our Barbie-doll craze threatened to grip the land, Mrs. Dodge devoted her monthly "Jack-in-the-Pulpit" column to setting her girl readers' values straight:

> No real, motherly, doll-loving little girls—unless their heads are turned by the folly of their elders—wish to have their doll-baby a stiff little figure of a full-dressed fashionable lady, flounced and curled, with perfume on her little *real* lace pocket handkerchief and a miniature eye-glass dangling from her absurd little belt. Now, do they?

It would be refreshing today to hear such a voice of reason and conviction on the subject of "training brassieres" for girls of ten.

Because the world seemed to offer unlimited opportunity for material and spiritual fulfillment, neither adult nor child then was likely to feel sympathy for the young ne'er-do-well of this *St. Nicholas* verse saga:

> He berated his luck—'tis the lazy man's way—
> That his profits were small and his rent was to pay,
> And he never once thought that his shortness of pelf
> Was due, not to fortune, but just to himself.

If a certain smugness was forgivable, given the optimism of the times, there were blind spots, endemic to all exclusive clubs, that seem remarkably insensitive in our less certain world today. Thus, Mrs. Dodge herself could write in another "Jack-in-the-Pulpit" column:

I don't know when I've laughed inwardly more than I did at a book that a dear little girl had in our meadow yesterday— [a Scribner title, *The Ten Little Niggers*]—and I'll tell you the thrilling story it illustrates, if you'll allow me to change one little word throughout the poem. So as not to hurt anybody's feelings.

At its best, within the family circle, *St. Nicholas* could not be faulted, and when, in December 1876, Mrs. Dodge prevailed upon her old friend William Cullen Bryant to write a reminiscent essay, "Boys of My Boyhood," it was like listening to grandfather tell of his childhood:

The boys of the generation to which I belonged—that is to say, who were born in the last years of the last century or the earliest of this—were brought up under a system of discipline which puts a far greater distance between parents and their children than now exists. The parents seemed to think this necessary in order to secure obedience. They were believers in the old maxim that familiarity breeds contempt.

But American society was changing rapidly and by the time William Fayal Clarke took over *St. Nicholas* in 1905, the nation's population was far higher than in the '70s and '80s, and of a changed character as a result of the immigration of the '90s. The machine age, just begun in the mid-nineteenth century and at that

27

time still of human, almost romantic proportions, to judge by
St. Nicholas' early stories about railroading, had begun to change
the face and character of largely rural America. Cross-country
communication was easier and the printed word, more readily
accessible, became less valued. The magazine carried stories now
on "Banking for Boys and Girls" and "Foot-Ball Under the New
Rules." The old *St. Nicholas* audience seemed neither so large
nor influential as it once had been. A major competitor even appeared in a revitalized *The Youth's Companion,* which began to
follow *St. Nicholas'* editorial lead, though its readership on the
whole was never to become so select nor its contents of such uni-
formly high quality.

Phyllis McGinley took notice of this gap between the two
publications' audiences in a verse:

> For I never read "St. Nicholas," "St. Nicholas," "St.
>   Nicholas,"
> The postman didn't bring it to that dear, unlettered
>   canyon,
> So the weight of shame is on my back.
> When I was young I lived, alack,
> On the other side of the railroad track
> And I read the "Youth's Companion"! *

St. Nicholas itself moved to the other side of the railroad
track in 1930 when its longtime publisher, the Century Company,
went out of business and it was bought by the Scholastic Publishing Company of Pittsburgh. In moving away from the old, well-
established cosmopolitan East to a metropolis created by the
industrial age, it was, in one sense, moving into the mainstream

* Copyright © 1934 by The New Yorker Magazine, Inc.

of the new age. In so doing, however, it more and more lost the sure editorial grip and attendant flavor that had made it unique. It had been *St. Nicholas'* great good fortune to come into existence at just the time when the nation itself was in the flowering of a serene childhood. The magazine mirrored the certainty and optimism of that stage of life. The world was fresh and new and everything was possible. With the Great Depression of the 1930s, the nation's and *St. Nicholas'* innocence was lost. In attempting to move into the age of mass uncertainty and mass marketing, the magazine expired in 1940.

SCHOOL is over,
  Oh, what fun!
Lessons finished,
  Play begun.
Who'll run fastest,
  You or I?
Who'll laugh loudest?
  Let us try.

K.G.

KATE GREENAWAY *Under the Window*

3: Greenaway Went Thataway

NOSTALGIA for the past—for one's own childhood or even for the fleeting moment—and a generalized sentimentality toward childhood and children are two quite separate phenomena. From the first have come some of the English language's richest books for the young: those of Randolph Caldecott, Kate Greenaway and Beatrix Potter, among others. From the latter come many of those books clucked over by doting great-aunts and assorted well-meaning adults who have, alas, long ago mislaid their own childhoods. By bringing a reflex coo to the lips or an easy tear to the eye of susceptible non-child browsers, books like Tasha Tudor's *First Delights,* Charles Tazewell's *The Littlest Angel* and Joan Walsh Anglund's *Morning Is a Little Child* help to perpetuate the unfortunate reputation children's literature has for prose of a marshmallow consistency and a life view corroborated only by the greeting-card industry.

The work of the nineteenth-century illustrator and author Kate Greenaway and the contemporary artist and writer Joan

Walsh Anglund provides superior examples of these opposite states of mind from which children's books may spring. Since both authors have in common many surface resemblances—the size and format of their books, the general subject matter and, above all perhaps, the painstaking attention each gives to the organization of her work and its over-all production: text, illustration and design—their differences are all the more instructive.

In each instance, the children of their books are presented as being out of some not quite specified past era. In Miss Greenaway's case, they wear a country costume half remembered from the small, rural town of Rolleston where she spent considerable time as a child and half created out of her admiration for late-eighteenth-century costume. Mrs. Anglund's children stare primly off her pages in an Edwardian, pre–World War I dress: middy blouses, boater hats, starched crinolines and super-sized bows in hair. Our attention, with both authors, is directed backward in time.

As important to Miss Greenaway as costume, however, are the particulars of the English countryside which she first discovered as a visiting London child and cherished ever after. Fields and flowers, orchards and hedges, houses and gently rolling vistas are all set down with lyric fidelity and made eternal somehow by the quaint timelessness of the beautifully clothed children and adults who trod lightly through them. The freshness of springtime, the clarity of country air, the lightness of the human spirit in such a setting—these are Miss Greenaway's subject matter. Mrs. Anglund's scenes, on the other hand, give no feeling of being particular or re-created either from memory or out of personal affection. Rather they are intelligent and artful assemblages, piece by piece, with an eye to creating a particular, calculated effect.

Her trees have had their foliage trimmed to the design require-ments of her pages. As a creator, she seems always to have one eye (or ear) out to catch the reader's reaction: "How perfectly darling!" or perhaps "Isn't that too sweet for words!" In Mrs. Anglund's *Childhood Is a Time of Innocence,* she places two small, doll-like children on a pond in a parody of romantic love ballads of a bygone era. Accompanying her drawing are the lines:

> It [childhood] is a timeless place . . .
> Where minutes are not numbered
> And the hours are sweet with happiness.

Surely no child would recognize his existence in such a generalized sentiment—more false than true—nor, for that matter, would any adult who deals daily with children. This overly sweetened and distantly idealized view—childhood seen through a rose-colored telescope—characterizes Mrs. Anglund's work, text and art. While both authors are consummate craftsmen whose work bears the indelible imprint of their personal styles, Mrs. Anglund's in-telligence is applied to the manipulation of her readers' latent sentimentality concerning childhood and children, Miss Greena-way's to conveying a vision of life.

Neither speaks primarily *to* children. They write *of* childhood: Mrs. Anglund in a way that uses children as a means of escape from adult realities which may not be so pleasing—the pain of growing old, the sameness of daily routine—and Miss Greenaway in a way that enlarges our appreciation of all green and growing things in nature—children among them.

This said, a child once introduced to Kate Greenaway via her *Mother Goose* or her own verse in *Under the Window* is likely to be hooked. "Children like something that excites their imagination—a very real thing mixed up with a great unreality like Blue-beard,'' Miss Greenaway once wrote to a friend. At first glance this seems to have almost nothing to do with her own gentle work. Yet, while she provided no exotic Bluebeards for her read-ers, the magic of her richly costumed children (a dress as un-familiar and literary to late-nineteenth-century England as it is to us today) appeals immediately to most children's love of drama and make-believe. What child's self-esteem or sense of importance is not greatly enhanced by seeing Miss Greenaway's solemn, grandly turned-out infants engaged in such wholly mundane and familiar activities as skipping rope, playing tag and holding tea parties?

The real difference in Miss Greenaway's and Mrs. Anglund's work lies in the opposing life views which inspire them. Behind Miss Greenaway's cheerful, idyllic English scenes there lies the artist's essentially tragic view of life. Her most sensitive biog-raphers, M. H. Spielmann and G. S. Layard, were aware of this when they recorded her adult recollection of Sundays as a child in Rolleston: ''. . . one note of melancholy discord on these Sun-day walks—the church bells, which from earliest childhood spoke to her of an undefined mournfulness lying somewhere in the back-ground of the world of life and beauty.'' She was more specific about this ''undefined mournfulness'' in some of her own letters:

January 1896:

Oh dear! Things are so beautiful and wonderful, you feel there must be another life where you will see more—hear more—and know more. All of it cannot die.

March 1896:

It's such a beautiful world, especially in the spring. It's a pity it's so sad also. I often reproach the plan of it. It seems as if some less painful and repulsive end could have been found for its poor helpless inhabitants—considering the wonderfulness of it all.—WELL, it isn't the least use troubling.

To Kate Greenaway, childhood was a metaphor for life at its richest and most bountiful. As an adult, she often recalled her early years with a nostalgia that bordered on pain:

October 1898:
How curiously days come back to you, or rather, live forever in your life—never go out of it, as if the impression was so great it could never go away again. I could tell you so many such. One is often present, I think I must tell that one now. Go and stand in a shady lane—at least, a wide country road— with high hedges, and wide grassy places at the sides. The hedges are all hawthorns blossoming; in the grass grow great patches of speedwell, stitchwort, and daisies. You look through gates into fields full of buttercups, and the whole of it is filled with sunlight. For I said it was shady only because the hedges were high. Now do you see my little picture, and me a little dark girl in a pink frock and hat, looking about at things a good deal, and thoughts filled up with such wonderful things—everything seeming wonderful, and life to go on for ever just as it was? What a beautiful long time a day was! Filled with time—

That shady lane with high hedges and wide grassy places— Miss Greenaway's Eden—recurs like an obsession in her illustrations. It is the locale of her world.

"What a beautiful long time a day was! Filled with time—"

Her work is fraught with poignancy not because she strains or in any way reaches for it, but because this awareness of life's evanescence permeates her whole life view. I can remember, with my own first child, experiencing such a sensation fully. Feeding my son one evening when he was no more than a month old, I was at the same time reading Lampedusa's *The Leopard.* I came upon the passage where the old prince sits watching a young relative dancing at a ball with the woman he loves. And the beauty and tenderness of the moment crystallize for him with the realization that they too—young, vital and handsome—must one day die. Suddenly, my son, lying in my lap, all innocence and potential, earnestly drinking milk, seemed an equally poignant figure. It was a pain, sharp and almost physical, to know that he, too, along with all things living, would one day be no more.

Something alive and breathing is at the heart of Miss Greenaway's world. When her "Little Maid" walks down the lane in *Mother Goose,* there is no question that she has a real destination in a real landscape and that we are merely privy to a passing moment. Children do not care "about children in an abstract way. That belongs to older people," Miss Greenaway once noted. Entirely devoid either of abstraction or condescension, Miss Greenaway's work appeals both to grownups and to children by virtue of its matter-of-fact naturalness. In her landscapes, children and adults alike are merely part of the architecture of her vision of English life. They have neither more nor less importance than roses or a blossoming apple tree. Take them or leave them, you can never doubt the reality of Kate Greenaway's scenes. Even at their most absurd (a state they occasionally reach), her costumes are so distinctive and convincingly realized that we suppress a smile in admiration of her unique vision.

It is not her draftsmanship which accounts for the effect she achieves, for, as John Ruskin, her most serious critic and mentor, pointed out, she drew shoes "like mussel-shells" and flowers that looked "as if their leaves had been in curlpapers all night." Yet he also admitted "the line is ineffably tender and delicate," as is the over-all effect, which, in those susceptible to it, is likely to linger a lifetime and, as Ruskin again put it, "alter one's thoughts of all the world."

The real world informs her every pen stroke and gives backbone to her work. "There is no charm so enduring as that of the real representation of any given scene," Ruskin remarked of her work as a whole, and Miss Greenaway's vision neither fades nor dates. England may one day be transformed into an industrial wasteland like the flatlands of New Jersey, but we can always return to her loving little landscapes for an authentic flavor of the rural English past. Her friend Austin Dobson once said of her drawing: "Her taste in tinting, too, is very sweet and springlike, and there is a fresh pure fragrance about all her pictures as of new-gathered nosegays."

If all is freshness in Kate Greenaway, in Mrs. Anglund all is artful contrivance—more like an Oriental dried-flower arrangement than an English nosegay. Mrs. Anglund's fabricated children, their faces no more expressive than Parker House rolls, sit or stand like display dummies in their made-to-order environments. Certainly Mrs. Anglund's tableaux have an immediate and insinuating charm. They are cute, occasionally even droll, and it is tempting to remember our pasts in such cozy clichés. Yet, by consciously manipulating her child characters to fulfill the requirements of preconceived tableaux of childhood, Mrs. Anglund stiffens and falsifies children. Her boys and girls seem always to be

JOAN WALSH ANGLUND *What Color Is Love?*

posing for us—on camera—in some way seeking out, and wholly dependent for their existence on, our adult approbation. Her scenes are ultimately cartoons, empty of any resonance beyond an immediate coo. Separated from life as we know it by an impenetrable curtain of sentimentality, they can appeal lastingly only to that sensibility which finds in the forced jollity and scrubbed pseudo-reality of the Lawrence Welk television show an acceptable and somehow comforting substitute for life.

It would be hard to expect much semblance of reality when Mrs. Anglund's children must serve to illustrate such imprecise and adult sentiments as:

> It [spring] is a gentle farewell
> to yesterday
> and the birth of new hope.

or:

> It [love] is the happy way we feel
> when we save a
> bird that has been hurt . . .
> or calm a frightened colt.

It perhaps says something of Mrs. Anglund's all-pervasive, sugar-coated sentimentality that even picket fences in her world seem always to have rounded points.

Miss Greenaway's airy landscapes, being closely observed from the English countryside she knew and loved rather than fabricated as backdrops for adult-inspired games of pretend, have the bracing flavor of ginger. By comparison, Mrs. Anglund's are more like treacle. The same holds true of their prose. Mrs. Anglund's thoughts are soft, imprecise, with blurred outlines:

39

> Love is a happy feeling
> That stays inside your heart
> For the rest of your life.

Not so. Love is an elusive feeling, for children as well as adults. Like quicksilver, it comes and goes as an awareness. "And a stone is brown," she tells us in *What Color Is Love?*, simply to complete a rhyme. "But it seldom is!" the honest child in us cries out.

For the sake of creating a pleasing surface effect, on the page or in the mind's eye, Mrs. Anglund is consistently willing to sacrifice the larger truth. Not so Miss Greenaway, whose nostalgic costuming and improvised child's play always serve to enhance her particular vision of nature and the poignancy of life as she observed it through passing seasons and years in the English countryside. ("Don't you think," she wrote of herself to Ruskin in a rare moment of exuberance, "it is a great possession to be able to get so much joy out of things that are always there to give it, and do not change?") Like her pictures, her own verse, at its best, was honestly observed and from life:

> When you and I
> Grow up—Polly—
> I mean that you and me,
> Shall go sailing in a big ship
> Right over all the sea.
> We'll wait till we are older,
>   For if we went today,
> You know that we might lose ourselves,
>   And never find the way.

One readily sees how Stevenson found inspiration in such work for his later *Child's Garden of Verses*. Miss Greenaway's children look forward. They do not exist merely as vehicles to corroborate a grownup's sentimental looking backward.

Mrs. Anglund's voice, by contrast, holds nothing of the child-like. Observing one of life's bleaker moments in *A Friend Is Someone Who Likes You,* she writes:

And then you think you don't have any friends.
Then you must stop hurrying and rushing so fast. . . .

Can this possibly be addressed to children? No, it is advice for the harried, middle-aged man or woman whose engagement calendar is overfull.

Even in her series *The Brave Cowboy, Cowboy and His Friend* and *Cowboy's Secret Life,* the stories—on the surface of more direct appeal to children—still exploit the fantasy life of the small cowboy for its easy charm rather than make of his imaginary adventures tales to interest other children. The series is interesting, however, for the insight it gives us into Mrs. Anglund's carefully cultivated visual vocabulary. In all three tales, whenever Mrs. Anglund depicts the small cowboy's imaginings, her drawings have an entirely different line, full of wit, bite and vitality. She does not have to draw with a pen dipped in honey. This dominant style is rather her acquired graphic vocabulary for imposing a particular vision of childhood on her audience.

Kate Greenaway might well agree with one of Mrs. Anglund's definitions of childhood in *Childhood Is a Time of Innocence:*

41

It is the happy hour . . .
The passing dream,
The tender time of innocence
That is part of us forever.

The difference is that, in Miss Greenaway's world, the sentiment is deduced after we have viewed countless wholly believable depictions of her airy landscapes filled with children, grass and trees. Mrs. Anglund, on the other hand, starts with a sentiment and then supplies severely edited, obviously ersatz tableaux to drive her point home.

As an interpreter of childhood, Mrs. Anglund is literary and didactic, a fact perhaps best explained by her own recollection of childhood: ". . . my happiest memories of childhood were the hours I spent tucked away in our great dark dusty attic surrounded by mountains of books." When Miss Greenaway spoke of her childhood, it was usually of herself in the world of gardens and people, outside of books, and outdoors more often than in.

Further, Mrs. Anglund tells us, "My illustrations always serve my idea—the words—to me the thought of the book is first." To Miss Greenaway, observation came first and her children fitted naturally into the over-all scheme of things as she viewed life.

In another of her many definitions of childhood (from *Childhood Is a Time of Innocence*), Mrs. Anglund says, "It begins with being born and ends with growing up." But the truth of the matter is it never ends in the best of people or in the best of writing for children. George MacDonald noted this in *The Princess and Curdie:*

There is this difference between the growth of some human beings and that of others; in the one case it is a continuous dying, in the other a continuous resurrection . . . the child is not meant to die, but to be forever freshborn.

This Kate Greenaway instinctively understood, and it is the constant resurrection—the springtime of childhood—that her work timelessly celebrates.

WILLIAM NICHOLSON *Clever Bill*

4: Blow-up: The Picture-Book Explosion

ICTURES are the most intelligible books that children can look upon,'' Bishop Comenius wrote in the mid-seventeenth century, and surely, since the publication of his *Orbis sensualium pictus* in Nuremberg in 1658 (which appeared in English somewhat later as *Visible World—for the Use of Young Latin Scholars*), publishers, authors and artists have adhered to his dictum both faithfully and profitably. It was not until 1872, however, that a full-color printing process developed by the London printer Edmund Evans heralded the advent of the modern picture book. For the first time, color could be reproduced, economically and in quantity, much as the artist conceived his work. The genre's first craftsmen—Walter Crane, Randolph Caldecott and Kate Greenaway—were thus encouraged and pleased to provide Evans with a steady output of art which, as it happened, was best suited to books for the nursery. Since the turn of the century, the continuing development of new and more economical ways to produce color illustrations in this country—spurred both by the photoengraving process and a population growing rapidly in size and literacy—has resulted in that embarrassment of riches which today faces every prospective buyer of illustrated books for young children.

A distinction should be noted at the start between illustrated books for children and the relatively recent picture book. Illustrated books have a venerable history, and their pictures, in most cases limited in number, are always illuminations or expansions of some specific action or locale detailed in the words of the all-important text. In this century, N. C. Wyeth was justly famed as such an illustrator. More recent examples would include England's Ernest Shepard, who provided memorable art work for Kenneth Grahame's *The Wind in the Willows* and A. A. Milne's Christopher Robin books, and, in this country, Garth Williams, whose spot drawings for E. B. White's *Charlotte's Web* must rank as inspired illuminations for that text. With the picture book, however, illustration assumed a new role: that of an equal partner in advancing the narrative thrust of whatever the tale might be. The illustrations in a picture book, always numerous, may well soar on flights of graphic fancy that the words never anticipated. The picture book, in fact, bears a decided resemblance to Siamese twins: the words cannot stand independent of the illustrations nor, in theory at least, can the pictures without text. Separately, their contribution is thin, incomplete. Together, they comprise a fully satisfying experience.

The modifier "literary" is best omitted from this experience, for the contemporary picture book is most clearly understood when viewed as a kind of halfway house between the seductions of TV, film or the animated cartoon and the less blatant charms of a full page of text. It is, however one defines it, a genre like no other.

Beni Montresor, the illustrator, has described the picture book as "a book whose content is expressed through its images," and he fears none of the literary consequences of this statement. "I am old enough to remember the accusations that used to be hurled at the cinema," he recalls. " 'Cinema is not Art, because, unlike the theatre, it does not express its content by means of words.' But who worries about this any longer? We all know that the cinema is based on images, not words; it is these visual images that give the new art its reason for being. Today, who can say, 'A film makes audiences lazy because it is made of visual images' or 'A film is intellectually inferior to a book or a play'? I'm speaking only of serious films."

If a puzzled parent should complain that picture books, serious or frivolous, do not encourage their children to read, Montresor has answered this too: "Ours is a visual time, a time of great and fleeting visions because it is a time of speed. One rushes, speaking less and less. It is the image that represents this best, and it is the image to which we most naturally respond."

James Johnson Sweeney said much the same thing a few years ago in his introduction to the catalogue of an exhibition of children's books: "A child's book is essentially a work of visual art—something that speaks directly to the eye and through the eye. . . . Its real role is that played by a Gothic stained-glass window in the Middle Ages." The comparison, while comforting to those engaged in the production of picture books, is not entirely appropriate. Gothic stained-glass windows of the Middle Ages were devoted to a single purpose which dominated the life of the times: the glorification of Christendom. The retelling of tales from the Old and New Testaments in visual images was a matter of high seriousness, governed by rigid visual conventions. The maker of stained-glass windows was in no way the enviable free agent today's illustrator of children's picture books has become. No subject matter is above or beneath his consideration, and no style prescribed. In fact, a seemingly insatiable market for picture books in our time has frequently resulted in children's books which the author-illustrator Louis Slobodkin once compared to "chilled lime gelatine, garnished with brilliant little bits of pimento—nestling in a few leaves of lettuce and tenderly resting on nothing."

The floodtide of talent channeled into the stream of children's books, particularly since the close of World War II, has assuredly brought with it an increasing number of works of superior graphic quality and immense virtuosity on the part of the artist. But often, too, there is little that speaks directly or even specifically to children. Of a great many such unquestionably beautiful books ostensibly produced with the young in mind, one could observe, as Arthur Ransome did in his review of Kenneth Grahame's *The Wind in the Willows:* ". . . if we judge the book by its aim [to appeal to children], it is a failure, like a speech to the Hottentots made in Chinese. And yet, for the Chinese, if by accident there should happen to be one or two of them among the audience, the speech might be quite a success." It is more often than not to such "Chinese" as may be buying books for children that their contents seem best addressed.

A case in point is a superior picture book of 1970 titled *The Inspector.* Created by George Mendoza (it has no words) and illustrated by Peter Parnell, it is a mordant commentary on the pitfalls of dogged determination in the line of duty, a horror story best appreciated by those with a long perspective on history. It is a children's picture book only because the genre has increasingly become a catch-all for gifted artists whose work is difficult to categorize. Many a picture book today functions as a temporary gallery between book covers for graphic artists whose versatility might otherwise be doomed to an occasional flowering in an advertisement or magazine spot drawing.

Nothing is easier for the adult browsing in a children's-book department than to become mesmerized and lost in the spectacular range of colors, clean design, handsome production and wide-ranging graphic ingenuity—what illustrator Henry C. Pitz has called "the polychrome of the present façade"—and forget that the object of a book for children is not to dazzle but to open doors to the child's own imagination and the wonder of the wide world (rather than simply the wonder of the particular production in hand). Just how frenetic activity has become in the picture-book field can be measured by thumbing through almost any recent work on the subject. Pitz's own *Illustrating Children's Books* (1963), despite its recent date, has not a single mention of many of today's leading figures: Adrienne Adams, Barbara Cooney, Ed Emberley, Maurice Sendak, Uri Shulevitz and Margot Zemach, to mention only a few. How is the book-publishing industry able to support this almost intimidating productivity?

The popularity of the picture book in this country grew only slowly during the early years of the century. Though such English writers as Beatrix Potter and Helen Bannerman (*Little Black Sambo*) enjoyed a wide success, the more elaborate and beautiful picture books of France's Louis Maurice Boutet de Monvel (whose *Joan of Arc* remains a monument to what can be achieved in the genre) were known to few. More traditional illustrators like Arthur Rackham and Jessie Willcox Smith dominated the early years of the twentieth century. By the late '20s, however, three eminently satisfying picture books—C. B. Fall's handsomely designed *ABC* in 1923; *Clever Bill,* by the well-known British artist William Nicholson, in 1927; and Wanda Gag's beautifully conceived black-and-white picture book *Millions of Cats,* in 1928— had proved widely successful, and the heyday of the picture book for American children, and for artists, began.

By 1930, new developments in photo-offset lithography made possible still larger editions of illustrated books at low cost, and publishers and artists began making increased and more sophisticated use of advancing technology. The '30s saw a great number of superior picture books bring the world, both here and abroad, closer to small children.

There were the cosmopolitan and colorful collaborations of the husband-and-wife team Maud and Miska Petersham, and Kurt Wiese's simple yet eloquent illustrations for Marjorie Flack's *The Story About Ping* and Claire H. Bishop's *The Five Chinese Brothers;* there were Munro Leaf's *Ferdinand* and *Wee Gillis* illustrated by Robert Lawson. In the '40s there came the down-to-earth and homespun books of Robert McCloskey—*Make Way for Ducklings, Blueberries for Sal* and *One Morning in Maine.* These picture books of the '30s and the '40s had in common their simple stories amply illustrated by straightforward and, for the most part, highly realistic pictures. There were few wild flights of narrative fancy and almost no graphic flamboyance. Perhaps the Depression and war years helped to keep down high-spirited inventiveness. Pictures followed text and the text exhibited an old-fashioned faith in the ultimate logic of events—the rightness

MAUD AND MISKA PETERSHAM *Get-A-Way and Háry János*

of the world—that has all but disappeared during the past decade.

As the picture book slowly gathered momentum during the '30s and '40s, its potential audience was growing to meet the new production capabilities of book publishers. The dramatic rise in the birth rate after World War II, combined with an educational trend that sent children to nursery school earlier but taught them to read later, meant more picture-book viewers over a longer span of time than ever before. Also, the popularity first of the comic book and animated cartoon and later of television unquestionably made postwar children more receptive to visual stimuli than earlier generations had been.

More often than not, printing innovations were developed in response to needs of the fields of commercial art and advertising, particularly during the war years when paper shortages strictly curtailed the output of new books. It is not surprising, then, that commercial artists became most familiar with the new machinery's flexibility and possibilities. Also, because the preparation of art for these new processes was often complicated and specialized work, the necessary technical competence was most readily gained in advertising and commercial art. There began to occur, in any event, a noticeable play back and forth between the world of commerce and children's books. One obvious result has been a rise in the level of visual sophistication required by the viewer of the contemporary picture book.

At the end of the war, large numbers of artists began shifting their technical knowledge and talent into children's books. Pitz accounts in part for the attraction of the field by noting that "association with the eternal awakening wonder of the child's mind preserves it [illustrating children's books] from most of the tawdriness of the adult world." And, in his 1952 acceptance speech for the Caldecott Medal, the artist Nicolas Mordvinoff attempted to clarify the relationship between the two fields: ". . . one can imagine the field of book illustration as standing in a place by itself somewhat between the so-called pure art and commercial art. Although in its essence it is attached to the former, the production end of it relates it to the latter." Whatever the explanation, there is a decided carry-over of adult wit and sophistication from advertising to children's books and, conversely, often a recognizable element of childishness—of deliberate naïveté and artful simplicity—employed in the world of advertising. The commercial posters and advertisements of Tomi Ungerer have both influenced his approach to children's-book illustration and been altered by his experience and success with a number of children's books. The same might be said of André François, William Steig, Joseph Low and others.

"Once upon a time, long, long ago," began Maud Petersham, documenting a migration that became increasingly common as the '30s and then the '40s passed, "after we respectively said good-bye to the advertising studio where we were both working, Miska and I started making children's books together." It is a tale that, with variations, can be told in the present by many another children's illustrator, from Leo Lionni to Dr. Seuss.

As increasing numbers of artists found themselves able to produce more and more spectacular effects with the new printing refinements, and as publishers found they could continue to offer the results at not prohibitive cost, illustration began to gain greater and still greater importance. The new picture books have little in common with *Peter Rabbit, Little Black Sambo* or even such '40s books as *Make Way for Ducklings*. The artwork of today's illustrator usually bears far more weight than the words

53

illustrated. With this assumption of the star role in the picture book, many an artist has begun to provide his own words, either from tried-and-true tales now in the public domain, old folk songs or nursery rhymes, or even his own imagination. This not only enables the illustrator to keep all royalties from his book instead of sharing them with an author, but it also gives him far greater freedom to illustrate as he likes, since he now has only himself to please. And this is where a large proportion of picture-book production stands today: a veritable Golden Age for the artist has made the genre increasingly alien territory for a purveyor of words of any weight.

Where once words contained nuance and shading, today it is more likely to be the illustrations that reward careful study. Hear Barbara Cooney tell of her illustrations for *Chanticleer and the Fox,* a picture book she herself adapted from Chaucer:

> How many children will know that the magpie sitting in my pollarded window in *Chanticleer and the Fox* is an evil omen? How many children will realize that every flower and grass in the book grew in Chaucer's time in England? Not all will be understood, but some will be understood now and maybe more later. That is good enough for me.

Blair Lent, who feels that children are interested "in the insides of things," not merely surfaces, provides for the books he illustrates small worlds complete. In his illustrations for Arlene Mosel's *Tikki Tikki Tembo,* the viewer can follow a mountain path from one end to the other of a Chinese village as the book progresses; he can see a winding stream from a picturesque distance and later cross over it by a wooden bridge. There is no question that Lent's illustrations require a more careful reading

BLAIR LENT *Tikki Tikki Tembo*

than the familiar and simple text they illustrate.

In many a picture book the importance of words is upstaged simply by the disproportionate space given to illustration. Even where a perfectly sound and absorbing story accompanies the pictures, the effect of the words is all but obscured by the scale and opulence of the artwork. Ironically, the Brothers Grimm, whose chaste and incisive prose is entirely capable of relating a story with high drama without the need of a single illustration, have proved most popular with contemporary illustrators. Uri Shulevitz has done an elegant rendition of *The Twelve Dancing Princesses* and Gaynor Chapman a strong, rough-hewn version of *The Luck Child.* Both Barbara Cooney and Adrienne Adams have embellished several other Grimm tales with their own visual interpretations. The stories are assuredly still there, but one scarcely notices the richness of the words any more or the subtle and economical twists of the narrative thread. Text now serves simply as captions for oversize, overplentiful and often overpowering illustration. More than once I have brought new picture books of old favorites of mine home from the library only to have my five-year-old son tell me when I finally sat down to read one: "Oh, I already looked at that myself. I don't want to listen to it." It is entirely possible that a generation of children is growing up undeniably quick of eye but impatient with and even insensitive to the sounds and meanings of words.

The new-style picture book certainly offers compensation for the loss in resonance of words. A few years ago, the illustrator Peter Spier, whose lively Dutch landscapes so enriched author Phyllis Krasilovsky's *The Cow Who Fell in the Canal,* embarked on a personal project of illustrating his own Mother Goose Library—"a new graphic approach to well-loved rhymes and songs," as his publisher explained. Spier's labors have thus far resulted in several books, including *London Bridge is Falling Down,* which can turn any observant child into a walking Baedeker of historic London as well as something of an expert on bridge construction; *To Market, to Market,* which re-creates a day in the life of an early-nineteenth-century farmer against an authentic background of Old Newcastle, Delaware, a pleasure for infant antiquarians; and *And So My Garden Grows* ("drawn on location" in Italy, as an extended footnote reveals), which is a veritable Cook's tour of Italian gardens from the Villa Della Petraia in Fiesole on to San Gimignano, Settignano, Rome and the Appian Ways, both old and new. The books are assuredly *tours de force* of some magnitude, but no child will ever remember a single rhyme after closing a Spier book. The Italian drawings, in fact, comprise more of an artist's sketchbook than a story and will delight knowledgeable adults rather than fidgety children. More and more, the picture book has become a vehicle for the illustrator's uninhibited self-expression. In indulging the pleasure of his own heart, he must often expect to be appreciated more by the adults who buy than the children who read his books.

In the hands of a gifted artist, often the frailest of literary wisps is turned into a visually rewarding picture book. Ed Emberley is one such illustrator, and his rich, inventive woodcuts provide many moments of pure aesthetic delight both in *One Wide River to Cross,* a free-wheeling adaptation of an old folk song on the Noah's Ark theme, and in *Drummer Hoff,* elaborated from yet another song. As graphic work, both are virtuoso performances, full of visual wit, and they provide a wonderful means of honing observant eyes to the subtlest of visual changes. Words are barely necessary and linger not at all once the books have been closed.

ED EMBERLEY *One Wide River to Cross*

In his speech accepting the Caldecott Medal in 1968 for his *Drummer Hoff*, Ed Emberley offered some insight into the craftsmanship of his contemporary picture-book production:

> The drawings in *Drummer Hoff* are woodcuts. They were drawn on pine boards, all the white areas were cut away, ink was rolled on the remaining raised areas, and a set of prints was pulled on rice paper. . . . Although only three inks were employed—red, yellow, and blue—we were able to create the impression of thirteen distinct colors. . . . By printing one ink over another, or "over printing," a third color is made. . . . The sharpness and brilliance of the color in *Drummer Hoff* cannot be duplicated by any other practical printing process, including any four color, full-color process. . . .
>
> You may have guessed by now that there is more to illustrating a picture book than knowing how to draw pictures. . . . The end is the printed picture. An illustration could be defined as a picture that can be printed. A good picture is a bad illustration if it cannot be printed well.

Clement Hurd, another illustrator partial to the design and color variations possible in block printing, seems often to forget the reader in the pursuit of technical effects. Both in *The Day the Sun Danced* and in the more recent *Monkey in the Jungle,* his elaborate artwork seems an end in itself rather than part of the telling of a story.

Margot Zemach's illustrations, on the other hand, often seem almost to blend into the texts, so beautifully do they fit a given tale. The rich red-and-brown illustrations, page-size, for *Mommy Buy Me a China Doll* make it hard to remember that the Ozark folk song long existed without their help. Her illustrations for

MARGOT ZEMACH *Mommy, Buy Me a China Doll*

Isaac Bashevis Singer's *Mazel and Shlimazel* are equally effective, though the story here, atypically, bears far more weight than the artwork. As an example of the complexity and sophistication of the illustration process today, hear Mrs. Zemach on this particular book:

> The illustrations for I. B. Singer's *Mazel and Shlimazel* had been done by a process which called for photoengraving the black line drawings and printing them on watercolor paper before adding the other colors.

The method used by Uri Shulevitz for his drawings in *The Fool of the World and the Flying Ship,* the Caldecott Medal picture book of 1969, seems even more elaborate as described by his editor, Michael di Capua:

> Soon he was working on an actual-size dummy of his picture book, a process that was to absorb him for some five months. When the polished pencil drawings for every spread finally satisfied him, they were reduced photostatically to half their original size; these half-size stats served as guides for the finished pen-and-ink drawings, which were then enlarged to the correct size. . . . This reduction/enlargement method was chosen by Uri to encourage the shaggy character of the black line. . . .

The illustrations of Leo Lionni, yet another sophisticated craftsman, could well stand alone, but his magical world of collage and color gains its richest meaning in the context of the simple stories he weaves around them, his "fables of search for identity and recognition." For a city child who has never observed nature close at hand—or for those children who seem able

LEO LIONNI *Frederick*

to walk through a paradise with unseeing eyes—Lionni's graphics are the next best thing to discovering the wonder of a blade of grass or a woodland fern all for oneself. No child should miss Lionni at his best—*Inch by Inch, Frederick* or *The Biggest House in the World.*

With the story increasingly subordinated to art, it is not surprising to find a growing number of picture books with no text at all. Maurice Sendak may well have sparked the trend when his Caldecott Medal-winning *Where the Wild Things Are* appeared in 1963 with a silent sequence right in its middle. For six wordless pages, his monsters take center stage and cavort, without any perceptible lag in the momentum of Max's dreamlike tale. The Swiss illustrator Peter Wezel has done two superior silent books for any child old enough to turn a page: *The Good Bird* and *The Naughty Bird;* and the Chilean Fernando Krahn provides a trio of beautifully realized visual fantasies of childhood in *Journeys of Sebastian.* John S. Goodall, in *Paddy Pork* and its sequel, *The Ballooning Adventures of Paddy Pork,* ingeniously uses half-page inserts to turn two silent works into charming motion-picture books, perhaps the last stop on the picture book's twentieth-century odyssey.

If today's picture books, having gone in many cases as far as they can go in a direction away from story-telling, fail to give children a rich store of literary memories or rolling phrases to fall back on at appropriate moments of triumph or stress—the heritage of those who read or were read books in an earlier era— surely they must result in future adults with informed and discriminating visual taste. It was the illustrator Robert McCloskey who noted several years ago that the picture book may well be a child's first and most meaningful introduction to the beautiful, and that it may even play a role in making future citizens more sensitive to the need for preserving whatever remains of our natural environment. If few would disagree with Pitz's belief that "a brilliant age of children's books is becoming the victim of its success," and that a combination of rising costs and audience saturation is encouraging exploration along new and possibly less flamboyant paths, the legacy of that age's best works will provide a rich and honest record for future children and adults, not of values or moral certitude verbalized, but rather of energy, versatility and sensibility as it was best expressed in our time: via graphic images.

FERNANDO KRAHN *Journeys of Sebastian*

ARTHUR RACKHAM *Aladdin and His Wonderful Lamp*

5: Rackham and Sendak: Childhood Through Opposite Ends of the Telescope

IN THIS CENTURY, no two illustrators better represent the opposite extremes of picture-making for children's books than England's Arthur Rackham and the American artist Maurice Sendak. To look closely at their work is to understand for all time the clear distinction between illustration and its specialized offspring, the picture book. Rackham, whose career was well launched by the start of the twentieth century, was, of course, never a picture-book artist. His forte was the memorable individual illustration. Sendak, perhaps the leading post-World War II picture-book artist in the United States, so totally commits his talent to the whole of each work he undertakes that his illustrations create almost a special weather for his picture books.

Conceiving of his pictures as "a kind of background music . . . always in tune with the words," Sendak is able to make palpable not merely actions but the psychological atmosphere in which they take place. "Where this kind of drawing works," he has said, "I feel like a magician because I'm creating the air for a writer."

"The writing and the picture-making are merely a means to an end," Sendak has observed of the finely wrought picture book. "It has never been for me a graphic matter—or even, for that matter, a word matter! To discuss a children's book in terms of its pictorial beauty—or prose style—is not to the point. It is the particular nugget of magic it achieves—if it achieves. It has always only been a means—a handle with which I can swing myself into—somewhere or other—the place I'd rather be."

Rackham's magic is of quite another sort. One imagines him taking the measure of the work he was to illustrate with professional detachment, much as a tailor might size up the idiosyncrasies of figure in a prospective customer. He then applied his considerable skill as an illustrator and fantasist to precisely those places which best suited his own gifts. The author's words stood or fell entirely on their own merits. They were of interest to Rackham only as prods to his pictorial muse. The narrative high points as well were strictly the author's concern. As an illustrator, Rackham felt free to let his fancy carry him where it would. Thus he often chose to illustrate the unillustrable, or to rescue from oblivion words the reader had most likely never noticed. From Dickens' *A Christmas Carol* he plucked the line "The air was filled with phantoms, wandering hither and thither in restless haste and moaning as they went." And he was one of the few illustrators of that particular tale who avoided the panorama of the Cratchit family's Christmas dinner as a rich opportunity for displaying his graphic invention. He was an illustrator propelled to his drawing board by phrases. The five words "taught them to fly kites," entirely expendable to the narration of Washington Irving's *Rip Van Winkle,* occasioned one of Rackham's most evocative illustrations for a commission that ranks with his best work.

Rackham's charm lay in the very adult matter-of-factness—the emotional detachment, perhaps—with which he went at each task. At their best, his entirely convincing, independent illustrations add considerable weight to the tale in hand. Yet, where the picture-book artist attempts to weave a oneness of spirit between illustration and text—in the process making a new and richer whole—an artist like Rackham cheerfully accepted the independent domains of words and pictures. His illustrations represented a kind of bonus, a gratuitous accompaniment in a separate medium to whatever work they adorned. Often, as in *Peter Pan in Kensington Gardens* or *Rip Van Winkle,* they were inserted as independent folios either at the book's end or in suites during its unfolding.

"Court painter to King Oberon and Queen Titania," as he was called by one admirer of his work for Shakespeare's *Midsummer Night's Dream,* Rackham could render entirely believable the most improbable scenes by pinning them firmly to elements of everyday reality. In his illustration for *Aladdin and His Wonderful Lamp*—a depiction of the vendor's cry "New lamps for old!"—we have no choice but to believe wholeheartedly in the wily lamp-seller's existence at precisely the place and moment depicted. Who could doubt the truth of that marvelous striped turban, the clothes so convincingly rumpled and those inspired Turkish slippers, at once Arabian Nights exotic and realistically well-worn. The conception is so natural, so precise in its mundane details, that we are almost willing to discount imagination as having had a part in its creation. Rackham was simply there

ARTHUR RACKHAM *The Three Bears*

and recorded the scene from life.

When we take Rackham's illustration for the traditional fairy tale *The Three Bears* and compare it with Sendak's work for Else Holmelund Minarik's *Little Bear* series, the difference between their two approaches becomes apparent. If we had any tendency as children to take *The Three Bears* with a grain of salt, it was because we already knew that bears didn't live in houses or eat porridge for their breakfast. Rackham gives us bears exactly as they would be found in the zoo, unadorned and unquestionably the real thing. Yet, there they are, at home in a cottage so lovingly detailed as to be, also, beyond question. Rackham scrupulously provided them with all the necessary household appurtenances: three honest-to-goodness crockery bowls; a squishy pillow on Mother Bear's seat (no wonder it was too soft for Goldilocks!); a checkered tablecloth; slightly disreputable scatter rugs on the floor; a painted clock on the wall, etc. We so completely believe in the existence of their cottage, as recorded by Rackham, that we willingly extend that credibility to the bears as its occupants. Rackham breathes, as his admiring critic Martin Birnbaum noted, "the indispensable note of actuality into his illustration." Another friend, Sir Arthur Quiller-Couch, pointed out "how definitely he gives us what is magical [i.e., the bears in an English cottage setting] . . . and contrariwise, with what a delicate sense of mystery he treats what is ordinary [the furnishings of their modest but comfortable household]."

The bears in Sendak's *Little Bear* illustrations are also real. The scale of the muted color drawings is modest, unadorned, as befits a first reader with a modest, unadorned vocabulary. In Sendak, however, our belief in the bears' existence springs from a different source: the reality he is able to inject into the rela-

MAURICE SENDAK (above) *Little Bear*
(below) *Father Bear Comes Home*

tionships between Little Bear and his mother and Little Bear and his friends. Chairs, tables, houses and trees appear as required, but Sendak's forte is making us feel, and come to cherish, the quality of warm relationships developed pictorially through an entire book, a sustained feat of magic of a quite different sort.

Neither Rackham nor Sendak depends upon color or graphic pyrotechnics for his power. Rackham's palette leans toward earth colors—a kind of moth-wing range of soft browns and grays, with occasional silvery gossamer effects. While not seductive in the manner of today's dazzlingly bright and bold books, his muted tones are somehow compelling—like a whisper that we strain to hear. Sendak too employs low-key colors. Much of his most recent work has been either sepia-and-white or black-and-white; and even at his most colorful (in such tales as *Where the Wild Things Are* or *The Moon Jumpers,* a single color, usually a subdued blue or green, will dominate. His predilection for cross-hatching also keeps his illustration on the stately and somber side. With both artists, it is the strength of their conception and its loving execution which give the work its authority.

That Rackham held in deep affection the material things of this world cannot be denied. He had what amounted to an obsession with fabrics—their texture and design—and could render them with a feeling akin to love that Sendak reserves for the psychological ambience of childhood. Rackham could use ten different, beautifully realized fabrics in a single illustration and still keep us interested in the picture as a whole. Yet that whole, oddly enough, had little substantive content. Like a vision or a dream, it is merely a crystal-clear evocation of a disembodied magical moment.

By richly adorning scenes of fantasy with the furnishings of everyday middle-class English life, he could render them totally believable. He once referred to fairy tales written down as ''consigned to cold print.'' His forte was breathing life into bits and pieces of that cold print as they struck his illustrator's fancy. He had a passion for oddments of crockery (the most memorable part of his depiction of the Mad Hatter's tea party in *Alice in Wonderland* is the Hatter's exquisite tea service) ; for the dressing gowns and slippers of old men (hardly a book he illustrated escaped having at least one dressing-gown scene—even *Peter Pan in Kensington Gardens*) ; and for cozy English interiors replete with rugs, quilts and bric-a-brac. Many find in Rackham a broad streak of philistinism, yet his logic worked: clothe a fairy being in a material real enough to touch and she, by extension, can be touched; she exists. At his magical best, he *was* the magical best, as when he uncovered Fairyland beneath the English countryside or lent enchantment to Kensington Gardens or Hans Christian Andersen's garret. What did it matter that his fairies were as industrious as the English working class or that they were engaged in the same sort of mundane activities—selling produce, winding yarn, mending clothes? (If he were drawing today, they would probably be found huddled by the ''telly''). He makes other, extra-terrestrial worlds exist for us, children and adults alike, and that is what really matters.

Unlike Rackham, Sendak is never distracted by the details of what his characters may be wearing nor the particulars of their objective milieu. He has said that it is ''this inescapable fact of childhood—the awful vulnerability of children . . . —that gives my work whatever truth and passion it may have.'' His illustrations, then, spring from the emotional reality of the child's world. ''During my early teens,'' Sendak recalls, ''I spent hundreds of hours sitting at my window, sketching neighborhood children at play. . . . There is not a book I have written or picture I have drawn that does not, in some way, owe them its existence." Nostalgia and pain—all entirely absent from Rackham's inventions—are often evoked by Sendak.

His quiet illustrations for Doris Orgel's *Sarah's Room* make us remember what it felt like to be small and powerless, unable to reach doorknobs and denied the privileges granted a senior sibling. Inevitably, we are drawn further into Sendak's world, more emotionally involved with each advancing illustration. In his drawings for another Minarik work, *No Fighting, No Biting,* there is virtually no developing action in much of the artwork beyond a palpable change in the psychological charge of the atmosphere as a brother and sister vie for the attention of their young aunt. Where Rackham's art takes flight into pure fancy, Sendak's remains firmly anchored to the deeply felt realities of his children's combined reality-fantasy world.

In recent years, Sendak has departed from the picture-book genre on two notable occasions: to illustrate two lesser-known works by the Victorian children's writer George MacDonald, *The Golden Key* and *The Light Princess,* and to provide the artwork for two Randall Jarrell fairy tales, *The Bat Poet* and *The Animal Family.* For the latter Jarrell tale, Sendak made landscape "decorations" of such surpassing solemnity and grandeur that they move beyond illustration into a realm of visionary art akin to William Blake's.

Though his drawings for the two MacDonald tales might almost be considered old-fashioned, neo-Victorian in conception and execution, the final illustration in *The Light Princess* is the quintessence of Sendak in his complete surrender to and self-involve-

MAURICE SENDAK *The Light Princess*

ment in the work at hand. The drawing is almost hypnotic in conveying the psychological tension between the heroine, that unfortunate princess without gravity, and the drowning prince, who has the face of Sendak himself. It is not an idle form of vanity, one feels, that brought about this self-portrait, but rather the artist's inner compulsion to become the prince in order to convince us fully of the tale's poignant moment of truth.

It is revealing to compare Sendak's enchanted, floating princess in this tale with some of Rackham's airborne fairy figures. Sendak's princess, decidedly of flesh and blood, is entirely terrestial. It is a suspension of disbelief to accept her as flying. Rackham's figures, conjured from pure fancy, take to the air as naturally as moths and butterflies. If each artist's work is considered as having an atmosphere, Rackham's is decidedly helium-filled, Sendak's a purified version of the air we daily breathe.

Nowhere is this more apparent than in Sendak's most recent picture-book dream, *In the Night Kitchen.* Though the small-boy hero, Mickey, is falling, floating and flying through space, in defiance of the daytime dictates of gravity, for the better half of the tale, he bears no resemblance to Rackham's disembodied creatures of the imagination. "Mickey the pilot" is a real-life little boy, full of free-floating sexuality and as yet formless fantasies of potency. When his anger at things that go bump in the night (while his mama and papa are presumably sleeping tight) triggers a marvelously convincing dream of power and glory, we are—hero and reader alike—simultaneously released into the warm and cozy world of the Night Kitchen. There, happily, food fantasies can still fulfill desires as yet without name. It is a tale that small children and adults who remember childhood respond to viscerally.

Chapter Five

It is a waking dream, with Mickey as the libido of early childhood personified.

Where Rackham's illustration is lighthearted and, in fact, lightweight, a gratuitous offering from a gifted but finally shallow adult imagination, Sendak's work is freighted with the memories of a solemn and even somber child. In *Higglety Pigglety Pop!,* his most personal work to date, Sendak has two illustrations—of an old-fashioned, horse-drawn milk wagon and an equally old-fashioned kitchen with gas water-heater—that give the feeling of having sprung full-blown from the artist's own childhood recollections. There is an element of compulsion, of underlying psychological necessity to Sendak's work that gives it its tension and deep truth. We cannot take it lightly.

With Sendak, then, we are summoned back into the emotional state of childhood, to experience its joys and pains as participants in every tale. In all that Rackham illustrated, he managed to maintain a cool, detached distance. Poring over Rackham's detailed pictures is like paying a visit to a curio shop or a quaint and unfamiliar house. Our visual sense is stimulated. We want to take in everything, but we are, in the end, untouched and unchanged, merely tourists—eyes drinking in the wonder of it all. There is never an emotional stake beyond aesthetic pleasure. By contrast, Sendak increasingly brings his considerable and constantly deepening graphic gifts to bear upon the subterranean essence of childhood itself.

6: Seuss for the Goose Is Seuss for the Gander

And on a day that I remember it came to me that "reading" was not "The Cat lay on the Mat," but a means to everything that would make me happy.
RUDYARD KIPLING, Something of Myself

D R. S E U S S, born Theodor Seuss Geisel, has won a formidable book-buying public by providing anxiety-filled diversion for listeners and readers at precisely the "Cat lay on the Mat" stage of development. As it often is in life, this anxiety is disguised and controlled by laughter. While his books are a far cry from what Kipling meant by "everything that would make me happy," Seuss has managed, almost single-handedly, to provide a safety valve for the overscheduled, overburdened and overstimulated child of modern civilization. In recognizing that children's craving for excitement, in their books as in their lives, is often merely the means for releasing pent-up anxiety, Seuss cannily manages to magnify and multiply the sense of suspense in his stories, not so much by the ingenuity of his plots as by a clever and relentless piling on of gratuitous anxiety until the child is fairly ready to cry "uncle" and settle for any resolution, however mundane, that will end his at once marvelous, exquisite and finally unbearable tension. The process is not unlike the blowing up of a balloon:

bigger, bigger, bigger and finally, when the bursting point is reached, Seuss simply releases his grip and all tension, like trapped air, is freed. If, as the British psychoanalyst Charles Ryecroft defined it, an orgastic experience consists of "a subjective sense of excitation followed by a feeling of discharge," then Dr. Seuss in his books—like Wilhelm Reich with his orgone box— can be said to provide his young disciples with a literary release not so far removed from orgasm.

Like many another illustrator and author, Seuss comes to children's books from the world of advertising. It was he who gave America in the '30s the battle cry "Quick, Henry, the Flit!" and breakneck speed has been his narrative hallmark ever since. His first book for children, in 1937, *And to Think That I Saw It on Mulberry Street,* was a prototype, low-key version of all Seuss plots and characters to follow. The hero, Marco, is—like his creator—a varnisher of truth. Despite his father's stern warning to

> Stop telling such outlandish tales.
> Stop turning minnows into whales

(precisely the talents that have won the book's author a firm place beside Edward Lear and Lewis Carroll as one of the inspired creators of nonsense in the English language), he cannot. Left to his own devices on a walk down Mulberry Street, Marco finds it impossible to suppress his gift for brightening up reality. From a garden-variety horse and wagon he sees on his walk, Marco compulsively builds bigger and better variations until he ends up with "a Rajah, with rubies, perched high on a throne" atop an elephant who, with two giraffe assistants, is pulling an enormous brass band, with a trailer behind—the entire entourage escorted by motorcycle policemen past the mayor's reviewing stand while a small airplane drops confetti down on the frenetic scene—all of it, of course, on Mulberry Street. Seuss's doggerel moves at a steady gallop and the artist's pen slides effortlessly from one outlandish embellishment to the next. The reader is at a mild fever pitch by the time the final invention is heaped on Marco's rapidly expanding universe. It is a blessed relief when the hero, home at last, is confronted by his fact-loving father's query: "Did *nothing* excite you or make your heart beat?" and he replies:

> "Nothing," I said, growing red as a beet,
> "But a plain horse and wagon on Mulberry Street."

Why does Marco grow "red as a beet?" Because adults, alas, are incapable of understanding what gives children deep pleasure, and it is always embarrassing to be forced to lie, even to keep the peace. The anxiety in Seuss's books always arises from the flouting of authority, parental or societal. It is central to the Seuss formula that the action of all his books with children as protagonists takes place either (1) in the absence of grownups, or (2) in the imagination. *The Cat in the Hat* performs his forbidden games when "Our mother was out of the house for the day" and *The Cat in the Hat Comes Back* only "when our mother went down to the town for the day." Young Morris McGurk daydreams *If I Ran the Circus* out behind Sneelock's Store without Sneelock ever realizing how pivotal a role he plays in young Morris' imaginings. In *Scrambled Eggs Super!* of 1953, Peter T. Hooper confesses,

> "Why, only last Tuesday, when mother was out
> I really cooked something worth talking about."

DR. SEUSS *The Cat in the Hat*

Seuss's books are obsessed with having "lots of good fun." What Seuss means by fun, however, is the sort of thing which, if it took place in real life, would place an anxiety burden on most children impossible for them to bear. Genuine fun to small children—like squeezing all the toothpaste out of inviting new tubes or taking apart Aunt Zelda's gift alarm clock—is always accompanied by anxiety because retribution is sure to follow. Only on rare occasions in life, therefore, will a sensible child yield to such temptation. But when the Cat in the Hat says, "We can have lots of good fun that is funny" (by which he really means fun that is forbidden), the child can sit back and experience genuine pleasure, knowing that the anxiety building up in him is vicarious and that no punishment will follow Seuss's forbidden pleasures.

Every detail in a Seuss illustration is calculated to add its bit to increasing the child's vicarious anxiety. Nervous projections and curlicues wriggle about everywhere. No drawing detail seems to be at rest. The hero of *Scrambled Eggs Super!* works in a kitchen where the coffee pot is ominously bubbling over as well as perched at a precarious angle on the stove. Milk glasses, filled, stand teetering on counter brinks; batter is splattered everywhere; baking ingredients are spilled. (And no cake in any Seuss book is ever intact. Large—and doubtless forbidden—slices are always removed.) It is just the sort of world no child's mother would put up with for one instant. The greatest pleasure in Seuss is derived from the sense of having a season pass to utter chaos with no personal responsibility for any of it. Seuss has a perfect understanding of grownups' love of order and the rule of their laws—and of the enormous anxiety burden this places on small children everywhere.

After the Cat in the Hat wreaks his havoc, the children's pet fish, a super-ego surrogate, warns:

> But your mother will come.
> She will find this big mess!
> And this mess is so big
> And so deep and so tall,
> We can not pick it up.
> There is no way at all!

Wolves and monsters be damned! This is the content of every child's worst nightmare. Seuss, of course, can and will clean up the mess with some magical last-minute plot invention, but it is the marvelous, wonderful heaping on of anxiety, almost more than the final release, that is Seuss's real success with children.

The denouement formula remains the same in *The Cat in the Hat* of 1957 as it was twenty years earlier in *And to Think That I Saw It on Mulberry Street*. Parents, burdened by household chores, the reupholsterer's unpaid bill and the compulsion to build character in their children, are incapable of taking a lighthearted view of spills, breakage and imaginative highjinks:

> Then our mother came in
> And she said to us two,
> "Did you have any fun?
> Tell me. What did you do?"

So, like Marco, the children tell her nothing at all—though they put the matter to a democratic readers' vote:

> Well . . . What would you do
> If your mother asked you?

There is another sort of Seuss book, no less subversive of authority, but in this case more of societal authority than the strictly parental. Stories like *Thidwick, the Big-Hearted Moose* and *Horton Hatches the Egg* take as their point of departure maxims which no child can attain the age of four without having run up against (usually because he has violated them). Seuss holds a noble sentiment up for admiration, then proceeds to turn it inside out. "A host above all must be nice to his guests," says the well-mannered Thidwick, and barely misses becoming a decoration for the Harvard Club wall in the adage's defense. "I meant what I said and I said what I meant," intones the upright Horton, "an elephant's faithful one hundred per cent," and everyone but he cashes in on this dogged virtue.

Sometimes Seuss is simply subversive of authoritarian rule in general, whatever form it takes, as in *Yertle the Turtle* of 1950 or *King Louis Katz* in 1969. What child will ever doubt that absolute power corrupts absolutely after reading of King Yertle's appalling *hubris* and ignominious downfall (the direct result of "a lowly burp" from the lowliest of his subjects, a turtle named Mack). *King Louis Katz* is a mellower and at once more revolutionary fable. By an act of open and willful rebellion, almost Marcusian in its purity, Zooie Katzenbein, the last cat in the line, shatters feline tradition in King Louis' realm. He simply yelled,

"I QUIT!
I cannot, shall not, will not
Lug this stupid thing around!"
He slammed the tail of Prooie Katz!
He slammed it on the ground.

And in one of Seuss's most satisfying conclusions—as up to date as student confrontations on the nation's campuses—he tells his young audience:

> And since that day in Katzen-stein,
> All cats have been more grown-up.
> They're all more demo-catic
> Because each cat holds his own up.

For all his exaggerated zaniness (and subversive alliance with the child's free spirit against all forms of authoritarianism), the ultimate moral Seuss presents is always sane and mature, one to which adults as well as children can subscribe. Though Yertle is undone, who can say it is not for the greater good?

> And today the great Yertle, that Marvelous he
> Is King of the Mud. That is all he can see.
> And the turtles, of course, all the turtles are free
> As turtles and, maybe, all creatures should be.

Though his sympathies are with the child, his sense of proportion is distinctly adult. This dual view finds representation in both pictures and text of several of his books. The early *The 500 Hats of Bartholomew Cubbins* starts out with King Derwin viewing his realm from the castle's ramparts and feeling "mighty important." On the following double-page spread, however, his small subject Bartholomew Cubbins sees exactly the same view in reverse—from a poor peasant's cottage down in the fields and feels "mighty small." The lowly turtle Mack, in *Yertle the Turtle,* complains:

> "I know up on top you are seeing great sights,
> But down at the bottom we, too, should have rights."

It is an adult voice, lobbying for the lowly, often forgotten child.

It is entirely possible that history will judge Seuss as the Patrick Henry of today's nursery set. Even where authority is benevolent and benign, as in *The King's Stilts,* one gets the feeling that it rests on wobbly foundations which ought not to be tampered with. The wicked Lord Droon has only to hide the King's stilts to bring the kingdom to near-ruin.

Another of Seuss's charms for children is his unfailingly direct language. In his doggerel, he has raised the vernacular nearly to an art form. Hear Mayzie, a lazy bird, complaining of her lot:

> "I'm tired and I'm bored
> And I've kinks in my leg
> From sitting, just sitting here day after day.
> It's *work!* How I hate it!
> I'd *much* rather play."

Or another vindictive bird about to flaunt her feathers:

> "And NOW," giggled Gertrude, "the next thing to do
> Is to fly right straight home and show Lolla-Lee-Lou
> And when Lolla sees *these,* why her face will get red
> And she'll let out a scream and she'll fall right down dead!"

It is a language children instinctively understand and appreciate for its honesty. It is the way people talk to one another: "the stuff people bake," "I sort of got thinking it's sort of a shame," etc. He is not afraid of contractions or inelegant phraseology. It is living language he uses to rich effect. Yet Seuss can turn a phrase with the best of authors. Consider his Grinch, a character unflinchingly mean because "his heart was two sizes too small."

Though there is a sameness of rhyme, occasionally even of ideas, in Seuss now that the number of his books is pushing into the thirties, his audience has not dwindled because the good Doctor's inventiveness of language and zany hyperbole never flags. There are few places where a child can get a better sense of the richness of language, the infinite possibilities it offers a lively imagination. Consider some of the new places Seuss has christened: Lake Wina-Bango; the towns of North Nubb, East Ounce, West Bungelfield, Yupster and Jounce; the Zweiback Motel and Foona Laguna. Or the letters he has added to the alphabet in *On Beyond Zebra* for children tired of the old twenty-six: Yuzz, Wum, Glikk, Snee and Spazz (indispensable for spelling "Spazzim/A Beast who belongs to the Nazzim of Bazzim"). He has given children and their book-reading parents birds as varied as the tizzle-topped grouse, the flannel-wing jay and the mop-noodled finch; and animals as startling as the seersucker, the stragglefoot mullagatawny and the Hammikka-Schnim-ikka-Schnam-ikka-Schnopp. There are also new taste sensations:

> And the yolks of these eggs, I am told, taste like fleece
> While the whites taste like very old bicycle grease.

It's hard to resist watching for what will spring next from the mind of a man who would feed an "obsk" a vegetarian diet of "corn on the cobsk."

In a day when children's books are almost unrelievedly beautiful and elevating, his are intentionally rough-drawn, tough-talking and almost downright ugly. They have no need to insinuate their way into our affections. A thing of beauty may be a joy forever, but Seuss is always a joy for whatever moments we choose to devote to him. At a time when the great majority of

picture books are a spare 32 pages—occasionally a lengthy 48—
his go on and on for 64 wild pages. Seuss's guaranteed audience,
of mass-market proportions, keeps production costs down and the
price of his books reasonable. We not only get our money's
worth, but are left with a reservoir of sane thoughts and an ap-
petite for his next outlandish invention. Long live Theodor Seuss
Geisel, physician to the psyche of the beleaguered modern child!

W. W. DENSLOW *The Wonderful Wizard of Oz*

7: *America as Fairy Tale*

Ev'ry giant now is dead—
Jack has cut off ev'ry head.
Ev'ry goblin known of old,
Perished years ago, I'm told.

Ev'ry witch on broomstick riding
Has been burned, or is in hiding.
Ev'ry dragon seeking gore,
Died an age ago or more.

L. Frank Baum, Who's Afraid

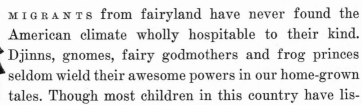

MIGRANTS from fairyland have never found the American climate wholly hospitable to their kind. Djinns, gnomes, fairy godmothers and frog princes seldom wield their awesome powers in our home-grown tales. Though most children in this country have listened rapt to such traditional tales as "Cinderella," "Rapunzel," "Rumpelstiltskin" and "Hansel and Gretel," surely the snug towns and virgin forests of early America could never have been their setting. Their heroes and villains, too, are decidedly denizens of another time and place.

A new people in a rich new land, our forebears directed their hopes toward the seemingly limitless horizons of the future. A bountiful fulfillment in the real world lay within the grasp of all. Few had time or need for the solace provided by fairy tales, those repositories of folk wisdom distilled from the disappointments and triumphs, the longings and heartbreaks, the wickedness and goodness of human beings from the primeval beginnings of the species. Long before the traditional fairy tale was frowned upon

91

by psychologists in the earlier years of this century, it was out of
tune with the freshly minted optimism generated by the New
World's promise. What had the citizens of a thriving infant re-
public to do with princes and princesses? The categories had been
abolished! And what real need had hardworking and ambitious
adults, or their children, for tales of gold amassed by miraculous
spinnings and spells, for sumptuous feasts conjured by magical
handclaps and wishes? In this land of plenty, riches were the reward awaiting all willing to work for them. And once the land had
been cultivated, famine was simply a Gothic specter from the
world's dark past.

The more lasting of our indigenous tales were of a different
sort: the tall tales of larger-than-life heroes above all ordinary
human adversity—Paul Bunyan, who felled the forests of the Far
West; Pecos Bill, who "got a stick and dug the Rio Grande";
or Mike Fink (he "made mountains quiver"), King of the River.
On the whole, life promised more than any fairy tale. What happier ending could be envisioned—not to a make-believe tale, but to
life itself—than that any small American boy might grow up to
be President or any young girl his wife? No glass slippers
needed, thank you, and no fairy godmothers. Fairy tales were
consolation for lives in need of magical solutions; but here man
was master of his fate.

In the 1830s a vigorous campaign was launched on this side
of the Atlantic, as it had been earlier in England and elsewhere,
to banish Mother Goose from American books for children because
"truth and instruction" were largely absent from her rhymes.
The crusade's leader, one Samuel Griswold Goodrich of Connecti-
cut, published a long series of Peter Parley books in the first
half of the nineteenth century to serve as edifying replacements

for the old fairy tales and nonsense verse. "I like matters of fact better than matters of fancy," one of Goodrich's child characters proclaims of his taste in tales, but Goodrich himself had a soft spot for Greek mythology, so the young man obligingly expanded his definition of the worthwhile in literature: "Well, if there's a sprinkling of truth in it, I should like to hear it."

Our first home-grown fairy tales were a nineteenth-century development and usually taken with a grain of salt, both by their authors and by their readers. But the essence of the old-world fairy tale was that its magical aspects be told with matter-of-fact economy and, above all, a deadpan earnestness that did not permit doubt, as in the Grimm Brothers' start to their version of "Rumpelstiltskin": "Once there was a miller who was poor, but had a beautiful daughter. Now it happened that he had to speak to the King, and in order to make himself appear important he said to him, 'I have a daughter who can spin straw into gold.' "

We are caught up in the tale's narrative thread before we have had time to consider whether it can possibly be true or not. (We have also unobtrusively been granted absolution for a common human frailty: the telling of white lies to make ourselves feel more important. "Straw into gold" indeed! Who of us has gone that far?) One of the charms of the conventional fairy tale was its casual acceptance of human beings with all their inherent imperfections: boastfulness, selfishness, sloth, vanity. The doctrine of the perfectibility of man, an outgrowth of the eighteenth century's Age of Reason, came too late to infect the traditional fairy tale, an inheritance from the oral tradition. It was, however, a key element of American democratic belief and subtly enters the fabric of most of our home-grown fairy tales and fantasies. The designation "fairy tale" is here applied to all tales that take for granted the existence of magical elements or beings in this world. The term ''fantasy'' is reserved for those tales in which magical realms may exist, but the tale's characters must somehow find a means of transport to them. The two genres, of course, frequently overlap. The folk tale, related to the fairy tale, is generally a story with legendary aspects, created and handed down among the people of a given region. It may or may not have magical elements.

The old European fairy tale was matter-of-fact in its clear-eyed cataloging of rank injustice and outright wickedness or perfect beauty and absolute goodness: they were all parts of life's intricate fabric. A father passively allows his lovely daughter to be turned into a scullery maid by a new wife; parents abandon two innocent young children in the woods—not once but twice—when feeding them becomes too burdensome a problem. The world, and man's fate in it, are full of uncertainty and surprise in these old tales. Virtue and hard work are punished as often as they are rewarded and, in some perverse way, this knowledge absorbed from the old tales always proves exhilarating, even liberating, for children. Such stories tell us that the future cannot be read with certainty, from nursery school through graduate school and on to a house in the suburbs. Capricious events may well bring unexpected alterations, for good or evil. The fairy tale's ultimate message is that there is a magic to existence that defies charting. And the charm of the best of the old tales lies in the convincing manner in which they record how bits of such magic can transform lives wholly: swineherd to king, miller's daughter to queen, scullery maid to bride of a handsome prince.

Yet, in most home-grown American fairy tales, no magic is ever more powerful than the overriding reality of the American life experience. The facts of existence always manage to win out over the fantasy of the author's tale. Surely this was true of Washington Irving's *Rip Van Winkle* (1819). The dwarfs playing at ninepins in the Catskills (and they are familiar, thoroughly Old World fairy-tale dwarfs) magically put Rip to sleep for twenty years. Yet the magic of their potion is not nearly so marvelous as the changes that come about in American life in the years of Rip's nap. When he returns to his old home town, King George's portrait has been replaced by George Washington's; and a new nation has miraculously been born while he slept. The dwarfs are entirely forgotten in the wonder of present realities. In *The Legend of Sleepy Hollow,* too, the magic of the tale is not that weighty sort which transforms lives. It is really no more than a glorified practical joke on poor Ichabod Crane, so that life in Sleepy Hollow can go back to somnolent normalcy without the irritant of the gawky interloper.

In *The Castle of Bim* (1881), Frank Stockton, one of the first and best of our native writers of fairy tales for children, introduces a magical hero: the loquacious Ninkum. This eccentric being can produce glorious feasts and even additional rooms for houses—but only with the aid of ready cash and carpenters, rather like the rest of mankind. His noteworthy magical quality is his ability to think "mind-expanding thoughts" about things that other people think cannot be. Chief among these is a quest he organizes to find the Castle of Bim, "the most delightful place in the whole world. While you're there, you do nothing and see nothing but what is positively charming, and everybody is just as happy and gay as can be. It's all life and laughter, and perfect delight." Before the tale ends, the Ninkum is forced to confess that he is not entirely sure such a place exists. Optimistic New

World spirit that he is, he simply feels sure that "there must be such a place; and I think the way to find it is to go and look for it." At this point, a sensible citizen whom the Ninkum has encountered in his travels replies: "You are a true Ninkum. I suppose we have all thought of some place where everything shall be just as we want it to be; but I don't believe any of us will find that place. I am going home." There are no permanent magical transformations in American fairy tales. No one lives happily ever after except by returning home with perhaps a new and deeper appreciation of the magic of his own day-to-day existence.

A still better Stockton tale, *The Bee Man of Orn* exhibits this same unwillingness—or failure of nerve, perhaps—to embrace magic fully and allow it to bring about some genuine transformation within the tale. The Bee Man is entirely content among his hives and honey bees until a junior sorcerer discovers him one day and decides the Bee Man must be under some enchantment to be living so solitary and eccentric an existence. He promises he can change the Bee Man back to his former self if only he can discover what that was. Thoroughly shaken, the Bee Man sets out to find himself. "It is not because I want to be better than I am," he explains democratically, "I have simply an honest desire to become what I originally was." After a careful search, the only being he feels kinship toward is a baby, and so the sorcerer happily returns the beekeeper to babyhood. This magical transformation is only temporary, of course, and the beekeeper grows up in time to be himself once more. There is neither escape from reality nor any permanent transformation in Stockton's tales.

Certainly this is true of L. Frank Baum's *The Wonderful Wizard of Oz* (1900) as well. The first American author consciously to set out to write "a native American fairy tale" (though he might more accurately have called it a fantasy), Baum begins with an American reality—a little girl living on the bleak Kansas prairie with a not-overly-cheerful aunt and uncle. Blown into the magical land of Oz by an entirely real cyclone, Dorothy brings a refreshing Kansas forthrightness to her subsequent adventures. She is a sort of American tourist in fairyland—eager, innocent and likable—but, despite the wonders and glories of Oz and the popularity she enjoys there, she is constantly homesick and seeking ways to return to her bleak Kansas reality. Indeed, the famed Wizard himself turns out to be an ex-balloonist from Omaha, an expatriate in Fairyland who also has a yen to return home.

Baum's stated intention at the start of the tale casts light on his philosophical attitude toward fairyland in general. "The old-time fairy tale, having served for generations, may now be classed as 'historical.' . . . The time has come for a series of newer 'wonder tales' in which the stereotyped genie, dwarf and fairy are eliminated, together with all the horrible and blood-curdling incident devised by their authors to point a fearsome moral. . . . *The Wonderful Wizard of Oz* . . . aspires to be a modernized fairy tale, in which the wonderment and joy are retained and the heartaches and nightmares are left out." Is this not precisely what our forefathers envisioned for their offspring's lives in the new world? A real-life fairy tale in which the wonderment and joy are achieved with all the heartache and nightmare left out. Baum's Oz books take place in a kind of child's version of the American utopia. The fields are always green in Oz; "no disease of any sort was ever known among Ozites"; "every inhabitant of that favored country was happy and prosperous"; and the Emerald City itself shines dazzlingly green through everyone's mandatory green-colored glasses. (It is rather like the vision of America in "America the Beautiful": "Thine alabaster cities gleam, undimmed by human tears.") And in Oz, as in the United States at the turn of the twentieth century, the magic does not really reside in persons, not even the Wizard, but in the material abundance of the land and the relatively smooth-running machinery of a government in which all the inhabitants fully believe. The Wizard's personal power rests upon his ingenuity and bravado—both thoroughly American rather than magical traits. If the Ozian utopia lacked refinement, smacking more of Barnum and Bailey than Old World elegance, it was not unlike America at that time: crude, perhaps, but filled with energy and a sense of radiant power and hope.

Possibly the most strikingly American quality about Baum's Oz books (and his *Magical Monarch of Mo* and *The Master Key* as well) is their idealism. The essence of the old-time fairy tale, as Mary McCarthy perceptively noted in *The Stones of Venice,* is its complete and unabashed venality: the shameless pursuit of gold, jewels, wealth and power. Yet, in no Baum tale is the quest of his characters for material possessions. (This held no exotic charm for American readers. It was too readily attainable in life.) Rather they seek courage, knowledge, a heart, adventure, or simply to find the route back home.

In the end, whatever magic the Wizard of Oz possesses, beyond his genius for gadgetry, is of a thoroughly practical, homespun sort, stemming from his life experience. When the Scarecrow demands his promised brains, even after the Wizard has been exposed as a fraud, the old man tells him honestly: "You don't need them. You are learning something every day. A baby has brains, but it doesn't know much. Experience is the only thing that brings knowledge, and the longer you are on earth the more experience you are sure to get.''

Magic is, in the final analysis, no more than good, plain American common sense. And it is this innate streak of common sense which has been both the hallmark and limitation of the American fairy tale. In another Baum story, *The Master Key; An Electrical Fairy Tale,* thoroughly American attitudes of democracy and fair play prevent the boy hero from enjoying magical powers bestowed on him by the Demon of Electricity. Rejecting the gift of flight, he cries: ''What right has one person to fly through the air while all his fellow-creatures crawl over the earth's surface?'' And he declines even more wonderful gifts because, as the author explains, ''he was born and reared a hearty, healthy American boy, with a disposition to battle openly with the world and take his chances equally with his fellows, rather than be placed in such an exclusive position.''

The tale is interesting on other counts, not the least of which is Baum's accurate prediction of several future electrical developments, including both the wireless and television. Of this fairy tale, he wrote in its preface: ''Here is a fairy tale founded upon the wonders of electricity . . . yet when my readers shall have become men and women my story may not seem to their children like a fairy tale at all.'' On several counts he was absolutely right. American ingenuity could equal and surpass the supposed magic of any imagined fairyland.

Spurred on to create still newer and better American fairy tales after the reception given *The Wonderful Wizard of Oz,* Baum published, in 1901, a collection titled *Baum's American Fairy Tales: Stories of Astonishing Adventures of American Boys and Girls with the Fairies of Their Native Land.* As his admirer James Thurber later wrote, "His American fairy tales, I am sorry to tell you, are not good fairy tales. The scene of the first one is the attic of a house 'on Prairie Avenue, in Chicago.' It never leaves there for any wondrous, faraway realm."

That curious confusion that seems so often to occur in American fairy tales between the world of fantasy and the wondrous realities of American existence is exemplified in Baum's own life history. After the great success of his Oz books, he moved from Chicago, where he had lived for some years, to Hollywood, for the purpose of becoming his own film-maker of Oz. There he also bought an island off the California coast—Pedloe Island—which he intended to turn into a real-life land of Oz for the children of the United States. This visionary plan never came to fruition in his lifetime, though a latter-day adventurer into fairyland American-style—Walt Disney—inherited Baum's dream and at last, in the 1950s, created a mundane, palpable fairyland, curiously combining elements of fantasy with re-created realities of an earlier America—the only fairyland Americans have thus far wholeheartedly embraced.

In trying to analyze the immense popularity of his father's books in the early years of the present century, Baum's son wrote, long after the author's death: "A disquieting gulf was growing between the new rich and the new poor; the cities knew the problems of the slums; and the farmers felt an unaccustomed financial stress." For the first time in our history, Baum's son felt, Americans were thirsting for utopias in books, sensing perhaps that these were not so readily attainable in life as once believed. During the period between 1888 and 1900—often labeled "The Gilded Age"—more than sixty utopian novels for adults were published, including Edward Bellamy's *Looking Backward.*

Oddly, these years of disillusionment for the many were the same ones that saw the most extravagant display of wealth and high living by a few Americans. The fairy tale became reality indeed, as a procession of triumphant merchant princes began to uproot entire European castles, stone by stone, and transplant them to these shores for use as private homes. On another level, however, these same closing years of the nineteenth century found quite different believers in America as fairyland: the immigrants from Southern and Eastern Europe, eager to seek their fortunes in the by now fabled land of opportunity. My own maternal grandfather, who came from Russia in his early twenties, confessed unashamedly to half-believing that the streets here were paved with gold. He often told his grandchildren how his heart sank on first viewing the cobblestoned streets of New York and finding them not greatly different from those in the small cities of the Ukraine.

In *The Rise of David Levinsky* (1917) the novelist Abraham Cahan documents this magical view of America: "My intention was to take a long stroll, as much in the hope of coming upon some windfall as for the purpose of taking a look at the great American city. Many of the letters that came from the United States to my birthplace before I sailed had contained a warning not to imagine that America was a 'land of gold' and that treasure might be had in the streets of New York for the picking. But these warnings had only the effect of lending vividness to my image of an American street as a thoroughfare strewn with nuggets of the precious metal. Symbolically speaking, this was the idea one had of the 'land of Columbus.' "

While it lay within the democratic realm of possibility to live happily ever after in real life, the American fairy tale was a

101

genre with few practitioners. And it is probably not coincidence that during the 1930s, the years of the Great Depression, Ireene Wicker, "The Singing Lady," gained national fame bringing the old-time fairy tales nightly into every American home with both a child and a radio. She remained wary of wickedness unvarnished, however—an American trait to this day—and her wolf was never allowed to digest Grandma or Little Red Riding Hood, and Cinderella's wicked stepsisters ultimately repented of their selfish ways.

With James Thurber's *Many Moons* (1943), a high-water mark for the American optimistic, common-sense fairy tale was reached. His heroine, the Princess Lenore, is languishing for want of her heart's desire, which is, alas, the moon. (It is a typically American wish: romantic, over-extended perhaps, but without venal motive.) Conventional storybook recourse to Lord High Chamberlain, Royal Wizard and Royal Mathematician is fruitless, for these stuffy retainers—encyclopedias of knowledge—easily prove the task impossible. The court jester alone, possessed of a thoroughly New World streak of ingenious practicality, realizes that the wisher must be taken into account as well as what is wished. He thereby devises the liberating and democratic formula that "the moon must be just as large and as far away as each person thinks it is," and he discovers that the Princess Lenore thinks it is not quite as big as her thumbnail, is made of pure gold and can be captured by climbing a cherry tree outside her royal bedroom window, where it gets caught each night in the upper branches. If there is a moral, it is a thoroughly American one: there is a practical fulfillment, surpassing magic, to almost any human desire once it is understood. With a little optimism, know-how and an understanding heart, wishes can be satisfied almost

as readily as any other consumer need. (The Peace Corps was
established with a philosophy not qualitatively different.) As
befits the heroine of an American tale, the Princess is in no way
upset to see the moon still shining in the heavens the night after
she has received her heart's desire. Just as children get new
teeth and unicorns can grow new horns, so too the moon renews
itself nightly. There are moons enough for all who may covet
them, and reality, once more, triumphs over fantasy.

Later Thurber fairy tales, such as *The Thirteen Clocks*
(1950), are marred for purist fairy-tale fans by the author's
overly flippant, tongue-in-cheek attitude toward the genre, his
flamboyant indulgence in puns and plays on words. "He did not
wish to give her hand in marriage," Thurber reports of a wicked
duke who refuses to find a husband for a nubile niece, "since her
hand was the only warm hand in the castle." And he treats with
unconscionable levity the predicament of a king caught in a wolf
trap: "I am no longer ert," wails the king, "for I have lost my
ertia." As for evil, always treated with utmost respect and
seriousness as an inescapable fact of life in the traditional fairy
tale, Thurber has his black-hearted Duke of *The Thirteen Clocks*
explain: "We all have flaws, and mine is being wicked." But
wickedness regarded as a "flaw" is somehow stripped of all
menace and authority as evil. Flaws are reparable (as in another line from "America the Beautiful": "America, America,
God mend thine every flaw"). There is in the American fairy tale
none of that unalterable wickedness so common in European
tales, a wickedness which requires real and powerful magic to
vanquish. In few American fairy tales is evil ever squarely faced.
The Wicked Witch in Baum's *The Wonderful Wizard of Oz* has
only to be splashed with water to melt away; and, in any event,

we learn at the book's close that Dorothy could not have been harmed because she is protected by "the Power of Good and that is greater than the Power of Evil." There was never any feeling in the old fairy tales, however, of Good being more powerful than Evil. It was the very evenness of the match which gave these tales their powerful narrative hold over the reader. Through the years, Americans have always been somewhat reluctant about giving wickedness its due. As the editors of a recent Frank Stockton anthology noted of his characters: "They are good souls living in a benign world, and the best of them are incurable optimists . . . evil is always tame and rarely enters his world." And Thurber's wicked Duke of *The Thirteen Clocks* is, of course, a horse-opera character despite his threats to slit any enemy from "his guggle to his zatch." His vaunted cruelty is meant to arouse no emotion stronger than laughter in the reader:

> Hark, hark, the dogs do bark.
> The Duke is fond of kittens.
> He likes to take their insides out
> And use their fur for mittens.

The American experience, until recent times, has not encouraged a bleak view of human nature. Since the close of World World II, however, there has crept into both American fairy tales and fantasies for children clear signs of a waning of New World optimism and innocence. There is less ebullience, a growing awareness of the limitations of even an abundant reality's ability to provide "happily ever after" endings.

In E. B. White's fairy tale *Stuart Little* (1945), his first book for children, the mouse-child hero, Stuart, is the second son of an otherwise perfectly ordinary American family. "The doctor was delighted with Stuart and said that it was very unusual for an American family to have a mouse.'' Most unusual, and it is possible to read into Stuart's unexpected arrival an unconscious metaphor for the scaling down of grandiose American hopes and expectations, for ourselves and our children, that began to occur in American life at that time. Other incidents in the tale offer corroboration for such a view. During his brief stint as a substitute schoolteacher, Stuart suggests to his class that they ''talk about the King of the World,'' amended (when the children object to the title as being hopelessly old-fashioned) to ''the Chairman of the World.'' When Stuart suggests he would like the job himself, one of his students quickly points out that he is too small. '' 'Oh, fish feathers!' said Stuart. 'Size has nothing to do with it. It's temperament and ability that count. The Chairman has to have ability and he must know what's important. How many of you know what's important?' '' The answers Stuart accepts are ''A shaft of sunlight at the end of a dark afternoon, a note in music, and the way the back of a baby' neck smells if its mother keeps it tidy.'' Surely such priorities, appropriate to a mouse-child if not to Pecos Bill, would not have ranked so high a generation or two earlier in the American experience.

In White's *Charlotte's Web* (1952), far more rounded and satisfactory a modern fairy tale, the pig hero, Wilbur, has only one dream in life: to keep from being turned into smoked bacon and ham when the cold weather sets in. Even as a piglet, he rejects the goose's high-flown adage that ''An hour of freedom is worth a barrel of slops,'' and neither freedom nor adventure is as important to him as comfort, friendship and the magic of simply living from day to day in a barn that ''had a sort of peaceful smell—as though nothing bad could happen ever again in the world.'' A thoroughly post-World War II pig in attitude, Wilbur is enabled to achieve his dream when his wise friend, the spider Charlotte, applies the magic of modern American advertising technique to his plight. Here again, the fairy tale reflects a new American attitude. Unbounded faith in the future is replaced by satisfaction with a comfortable and familiar *status quo*. An imperfect reality is magic enough for Wilbur.

The Phantom Tollbooth, Norbert Juster's first-rate fantasy of 1967, relates the strange adventures of a small boy, Milo, who, far from being content with contemporary American urban life, is suffering from a junior case of *anomie*. '' 'It seems to me that almost everything is a waste of time,' he remarked one day as he walked dejectedly home from school. 'I can't see the point in learning to solve useless problems, or subtracting turnips from turnips, or knowing where Ethiopia is or how to spell February . . . and worst of all,' he continued sadly, 'there's nothing for me to do, nowhere I'd care to go, and hardly anything worth seeing.' '' By means of a magical ''genuine turnpike tollbooth,'' he embarks on a journey toward understanding which at many points seems seriously to question long unexamined certitudes of American life. Milo travels beyond Expectations (a journey few American children before his time ever thought to make) into a land of make-believe, Wisdom, discovered long ago and settled on what sound like New World high principles. (''Then one day a small ship appeared on the Sea of Knowledge. It carried a young prince seeking the future. In the name of goodness and truth he laid claim to all the country and set out to explore his new domain.'') The land has fallen on evil days, alas, because the sisters Rhyme and Reason have been wrongheadedly banished from its shores, and Milo accepts the task of bringing them back. In the course of his quest, he learns many useful lessons: that "the most important reason for going from one place to another is to see what's in between"; that "just because you have a choice, it doesn't mean that any of them *has* to be right"; and that it is sometimes possible, if being fed "subtraction stew," to eat more and more and yet grow hungrier and hungrier. Milo ultimately succeeds in his job, but only because no one has bothered to inform him in advance of what everyone knew: "It was impossible." Armed with new knowledge from this magical realm, he returns home with hopes of making more sense of the reality he has always known. It is a bittersweet tale in which everyday life comes off rather poorly.

The late 1960s have also brought a wave of bittersweet fairy and folk tales to readers and listeners at the youngest age level. It cannot be simply accident that many of them, even for the youngest children, confront the question "What is happiness?" As E. B. White once noted, "Like toys, books for children reflect surely the temper of the period into which they are born." And the temper of the '50s and '60s in the United States has moved steadily away from unexamined faith in democracy, justice, equality, opportunity for all and the Panglossian notion that "all is for the best in this best of all possible worlds." In children's literature as well as on the college campuses of the nation, a late-blooming malaise is rampant.

In William Steig's fairy tale *Sylvester and the Magic Pebble,* which won the Caldecott Medal for 1969, a rock-collecting young donkey discovers a magic red pebble which fulfills his every wish. "Anybody at all can have everything anybody wants" (a reasonably accurate approximation of the American dream), he realizes; but before he is able to put his revelation to any practical use, he carelessly wishes himself into a stone to avoid being eaten by a lion. Dropping his magic pebble in the process, Sylvester moves instantaneously from having everything to having nothing. Finally turned back into himself by virtue of luck and the loyalty and love of his parents, he realizes that simply to be alive and cherished is the greatest happiness of all.

William Wondriska's *Mr. Brown and Mr. Gray* (1968) finds a horse king wistfully confronting two of his subject pigs with the direct question: "Do you know what happiness is?" One subject, Mr. Brown, is certain that, given the wherewithal to acquire his heart's desire, he will be able to give the king an answer. The king grants each subject his own island and *carte blanche* to do as he will with it for one year. Mr. Brown becomes history's most conspicuous consumer: buying yachts, cars, 365 television sets, planes, a swimming pool and a luxury hotel. Mr. Gray cheerfully moves his wife and family to his island, lives simply, plants a vegetable garden and flowers, swims and thoroughly enjoys the new situation. At the end of one year, when the horse king returns for an answer, Mr. Brown is no nearer a reply. If only *he* could be king, he feels, then he would surely find it. Mr. Gray, who had no answer at the outset, is also still without one, but the wise horse king realizes from the Gray family's life style that happiness is simply the capacity to enjoy what you've already got. He cheerfully gives up his crown to Mr. Brown in order to become Mr. Gray's neighbor in contentment.

Anita Lobel, who has provided a number of richly illustrated folk and fairy tales for youngest children, has, in *The Seamstress of Salzburg* (1970), succeeded in capturing the flavor of the old European fairy tale while at the same time turning the Horatio Alger myth inside out. Anna, the heroine, is an extraordinary young seamstress who makes the most beautiful clothes imaginable for the members of her own family. Discovered one day by the Duchess of Frutz, she becomes the darling of fashionable Salzburg. She receives commission upon commission to outfit the highborn ladies of the court, including finally the Queen herself. Anna's parents, selfishly delighted with the money and fame their daughter's talent is bringing in, and quite impervious to her growing fatigue and depression, urge her on. As in the old Alger formula, talent and hard work have brought fame and fortune— but, alas, no attendant happiness. Exhausted, Anna no longer sews out of love but rather like an overused machine. She forgets to complete seams and her dresses begin to fall apart. Because her shoddy, mass-production needlework causes the Queen high embarrassment on a state occasion, Anna is sentenced to be hanged. Fortunately, she is rescued by a handsome prince and then, in turn, Anna helps to save the court ladies of Salzburg from their own empty-headed existence by teaching them, too, to find fulfillment in creating something for themselves: their own clothes.

While M. B. Goffstein's recent works *Goldie the Dollmaker* (1969) and *Two Piano Tuners* (1970) are not, strictly speaking, fairy tales—they are more folk fables for our time—they confront the question of personal happiness in strikingly similar terms. In *Goldie,* an orphaned young toymaker earns enough from the fabrication of beautiful wooden dolls to live comfortably in her own small house in the woods, satisfying every material want. She suffers, however, from an overwhelming loneliness until she realizes that, through work lovingly done, one individual being can speak—across national boundaries and even the centuries—to all others who appreciate quality and craftsmanship. It is not what one is able to take from life that provides fulfillment, but what one is able gratuitously to give from within himself.

Two Piano Tuners is still more concerned with the particulars of what constitutes human fulfillment. Here the locale is decidedly urban United States. Mr. Weinstock, a piano tuner by profession, is bringing up his young, orphaned granddaughter, Debbie. Like all American parents before him, he wants "something better" for Debbie, more exalted certainly than being a mere piano tuner. He dreams of her becoming a concert pianist. But the child, full of admiration for her grandfather's skill and in awe of the mysterious powers of the tools of his profession, wants only to be a piano tuner, too. The moral of the Goffstein tale is that "Everybody should take the responsibility for finding out what it is he really wants to do" and that there is greater virtue in being a good piano tuner than a mediocre concert pianist. Parting company with the grandiose generalities of the American Dream— that everyone can reach the highest pinnacle of fame and fortune —the author stresses the inherent beauty and fulfillment of finding the right niche, regardless of its elevation on the status scale.

As profound an American fairy tale as has yet been written, though it has never been considered seriously in this light, is Maurice Sendak's *Higglety Pigglety Pop! or There Must Be More to Life* (1967). It begins where the traditional tale leaves off: at "And they lived happily ever after." Its dog heroine, Jennie, has everything—a loving master, two windows from which to enjoy the views, two pillows, two bowls—in short, all the creature comforts a creature could covet in life. Yet Jennie packs her bag and leaves an idyllic reality. "I am discontented," she announces. "I want something I do not have. There must be more to life than having everything." Jennie's lament brings her face to face with no less than the fallacy of the American dream: that man's happiness will be achieved when he has every imaginable material comfort. But if not, where can he turn for solace and sustenance? Jennie answers an advertisement for a "Leading Lady for The World Mother Goose Theatre" and embarks on a dream-like odyssey into a simpler American past via an old-fashioned, horse-drawn milk wagon with big wooden wheels. She enters a world of Victorian make-believe where "Mother Goose" seems to be the magic password. She loses all her former worldly possessions and comes also to realize that "There must be more to life than having nothing." Jennie finds her fulfillment (and immortality) by becoming the star of The World Mother Goose Theatre. Discovering one's own vocation—inner satisfaction—is better than having everything or nothing. The comfortable life is hollow and meaningless unless one occasionally puts one's head into the lion's mouth of pure fantasy, of dreaming one's own dreams, following personal paths that can lead somewhere or nowhere. Jennie's dreams are finally fulfilled in performing at Castle Yonder. But she writes to her old master, "I can't tell you how to get to the Castle Yonder because I don't know where it is. But if you ever come this way, look for me."

Thus we may have come full circle. Having long had a thin tradition of American fairy tales precisely because of a deeply held faith in the fairy-tale aspects of the American dream, we have in our time lost that faith and are creating new and more convincing American fairy tales and fantasies. And by exploring untried paths to the inner self, we may uncover new and richer meanings —beyond the materialism of the Old World and the New—to "And they lived happily ever after."

8: *All That's Golden Is Not Glitter*

WHEN IT IS impossible to find in the library, has never been mentioned in *The New York Times Book Review, The Saturday Review* or *Book World,* yet is lying on your child's bookshelf and finds house room in numberless thousands of dwellings with offspring under ten across the nation, it is a safe bet that the commodity in question is what in juvenile publishing today is designated a mass-market book.

There was once a well-known New York art collector who told all the gallery owners with whom she dealt that it was no use trying to sell her a painting. "I only buy those," she confided, "that say 'mama' to me." And perhaps the most meaningful definition of a *merchandise* or *mass-market* book is one that says "mama" to no fewer than a quarter of a million buyers in the course of its life in print.

This quality of instant broad appeal is, of course, both the antithesis of *St. Nicholas'* patrician call to a highly literate readership and a hallmark of mass-market publishing. Since literature has little to do either with instant appeal or with sales measured in six figures, there are those who would dismiss merchandise publishing without further hearing. The illustrator Nicolas Mordvinoff, winner of a Caldecott Medal in 1952, said of much of such work: "To please on the surface is no more than to attract attention by a bright display in the window of an empty store. It is a form of treachery. Art is life, and life is no candy." More recently, Robert Lasson, writing in *Book World* about the adult variety of merchandise book, noted: "It looks like a book, it has pages like a book . . . and it's sold on book counters. It must *be* a book. Wrong. It's not a book. It's a product. A product that slyly takes on the trappings of the real thing. A product is intended not to inform or to instruct or even to amuse but to sell. If the product is successful, it is a good product. If it fails, it is a poor product." Lasson's damnation can be accepted as a working definition—i.e., that merchandise books are products in book form. The observation may even be added that it is only a happy accident if such works also turn out, on occasion, to have literary merit as well as booklike appearance. With this as a starting point, the student of mass-market books has some hope of understanding a fascinating phenomenon of assembly-line publishing in our time.

The possible reasons for the selling power of merchandise books are many and often conflicting: a carefully calculated, well-aimed appeal; price; novelty; utility; availability; the buyers' naïveté; good value and unqualified merit all among them. The kinds of book which fall into the merchandise category cut a wide swath. There are the familiar Shape, Little Golden and Wonder Books which sell for under forty cents. There is a wide variety of semi-toy, semi-book items—the floppy cloth books with their zippers, buttons and bows that are supposed to help children learn the mechanics of dressing themselves; those plastic-paged novelties that can shed water like a duck and float in the bathtub (which is more than can be said for a surprising number of wooden boats on sale in toy departments today); books with orifices through which one can feel fur, sandpaper or silk; spiral-bound books whose pages separate like jigsaw puzzles so that one can make one's own conglomerate texts and pictures; and, most recently, books with "fragrance strips" that offer assorted smells. Then, too, there are attractively priced packets of minibooks (an economical use of odd bits of the large sheets out of which book pages are cut)—like Maurice Sendak's tetralogy, The Nutshell Library, consisting of *Chicken Soup with Rice, Alligators All Around, Pierre* and *One Was Johnny,* or Jean de Brunhoff's four elephant vignettes in *Babar's Trunk;* and a wide array of what to the untutored eye appear to be just garden-variety books with authors like Dr. Seuss or Richard Scarry, or such perennially charismatic subject matter as Christmas, a single best-loved classic, a hundred best-loved poems, a thousand riddles and puzzles, and a million answers to every child's most outrageous questions. All are seductively packaged and popularly priced so that they virtually leap off the book table and into the prospective buyer's arms. Almost without exception, the age range of such books is two to ten and their appeal is essentially visual rather than literary.

Golden Press, which produces between eighty and a hundred merchandise titles annually, recently acknowledged this prime importance of the eye when it acquired a new corporate logogram, the lower-case letters "g" and "b" in whose centers appear two targetlike dots, peering out at the world like small, round eyes. The motto "Children See a Lot in Golden Books" underscores the calligraphic imagery and makes entirely clear just where the emphasis lies.

Ever since John Newbery published his first juvenile, *A Little Pretty Pocket Book,* in London in 1744, it has been every publisher's dream to provide children's books that sell in quantity. Thus, no unconscionable venality lies in this goal. But merchandise publishing is predicated on the expectation and economic necessity of spectacularly high sales. Roberta Miller, a former senior editor at Golden Press and creator of that house's popular block books, defined a mass-market book as "one that will interest 300,000 children, selling out its initial print order in one season and continuing strong for at least two years after that." Where a normal first printing of the standard picture book at a trade-book house may run somewhere between 10,000 and 15,000 copies, the minimum print order of a merchandise book will be no less than 20,000 and occasionally as high as a quarter of a million.

What enables the merchandise publisher to sell so many books? To begin with, he travels an opposite course from his trade-book counterpart. In the latter case, an editor will accept for publication a manuscript he likes and then hope that his taste and knowledge of children, parents and librarians will help assure that the published work will find its audience. The merchandise publisher, however, often starts with a particular and fairly accurately calculated market firmly in mind, then tailors his books to reach it. "I would not do a book at Golden," Mrs. Miller flatly stated, "if our marketing man didn't think it would sell."

How can the marketing man be so sure of his judgments? While bookstore sales have a limited importance to him, librarians —so central to the success of the "quality" publisher's books— are not at all crucial to his thinking. It is the department, chain and discount stores that determine the success or failure of a group of merchandise books. The big chains—such as Woolworth, J. C. Penney and W. T. Grant—generally place sizable advance orders through their own central purchasing offices. From these sources word will reach the publisher as to what sort of book is moving. Content is likely to be less crucial than size, price and look. ''We are getting an amazing number of calls for $1.95 flats'' (large-format, flat-stacking picture books), one editor reported in the fall of 1969. Her reasoning for the upsurge of interest was that where the standard price for a birthday-party book was once $1, inflation had jumped it to $1.95.

It is characteristic of merchandise publishing that a single title is seldom as important as a series or ''line'' of books. Because the big chain stores buy books in bulk, they tend to favor an assortment of titles in a format that is proving to be popular. Thus Golden will put out its Shape Books by sixes and sevens, as will Grosset its 3-D puppet storybooks. Because packaging looms so large, there is a great deal of copying from one house to another, much more so than if distinctive content were the books' selling point. ''There's nothing we do,'' said one of Golden's top idea men, ''that another publisher can't duplicate.'' Thus Grosset, noting the success of Golden's Shape Books, quickly produced Sturdi-Contour Books of its own; and Golden, fully aware of what a good thing it has in the inexpensive, easily stacked Shape Books (sales are well in excess of 5,000,000 annually), began stretching the concept to include a *Peter Pan* book, a *Chitty Chitty Bang Bang* book and *101 Dalmatians*. Where the charm of the earlier Shape Books lay in the fact that the books' silhouettes were logical extensions of the material inside them (a kitten-shaped book told all about felines), the most recent titles have no logic beyond that of salability. "That's the trouble with success in our business," noted a Golden editor. "Either you are pressured by your customers for more titles in a hot line, or you begin yourself to get greedy and dissipate your own best ideas."

Since the look or novelty of such a book occupies more of the publisher's time than its contents, it is not surprising that the language of the mass-market book field often sounds more appropriate to the wholesale grocery business. It is not unusual to hear editors refer to the "shelf life" of books. Because quick turnover and volume sales are mandatory, the merchandise publisher must aim for instantaneous appeal. And the sort of book which sells on the basis of its outward appearance must be purchased in quantity reasonably quickly; otherwise its instant appeal, like an open bottle of soda pop, loses its fizz. "These books sell themselves," said a Platt and Munk editor. "They have great covers or marvelous titles—hopefully, both—and they hit home with that segment of the public that buys most books for young children." Platt and Munk devotes a good deal of its marketing target practice to parents in the age group between twenty and thirty-two. Other houses make a greater appeal to what is called the "gift-book market." Though the purchasers of many—possibly most—merchandise books do not themselves read much, they know that books, like vitamins, are good for children. If, therefore, books with beckoning covers and reasonable prices are available in the places where they shop, the merchandising omens are favorable for steady sales.

There is, of course, no simple over-all marketing formula suited to all sections of the country. Certain categories of book, known to sell like hotcakes in one area, will not even be marketed in others. Golden, for example, has *The Children's Bible,* a $1 flat, that is a best-seller in drugstore and supermarket outlets in parts of the South and Midwest. The fact that it is shrink-wrapped so that the buyer cannot even look inside before purchase does not seem to have impeded sales. It is a book that would be hard to come by, however, in either New York or Chicago.

On the whole, the staple contents of merchandise books are predictable. There are a great many undistinguished rehashes of fairy tales, the usual ABCs, *Mother Goose* collections, baby-animal catalogues and a wide selection of informational books often in question-and-answer form. It is not, in fact, unusual for a single publisher to have virtually the same book in several different formats.

"Repackaging" is one of the ways in which merchandise publishers are able to offer their books inexpensively. "We have a beautiful backlist to draw on," Mrs. Miller said of Golden. And it is this beautiful backlist which made it possible for that house to introduce a handsome series of nonfiction Golden Paperbacks in the fall of 1968, each 80 pages long, with generous use of four-color illustration and printed on heavy, bright-white offset paper, all for 75 cents each. The texts, with few exceptions, came from earlier Golden books in a variety of formats. More important, the illustrations were ready-made. "The longer you are in this business, the cheaper you are able to produce," the editor of the series pointed out. "The big cost in using four-color illustration is the making of the color separations necessary for printing." But once done, the separations can be stored and used, in a variety of sizes, again and again.

Repackagings take place at all price levels. Thus, a recent Grosset title, *Kittens and Puppies, Horses and Rabbits and Insects, Turtles and Birds,* priced at $4.95 and aimed at gift buyers, was simply a larger-format, better-designed amalgam of nine earlier Wonder Book titles which sold at 25 or 35 cents. Platt and Munk, a few years ago, brought out at $2.50 two highly successful color-photograph books for youngest children called *Things to See* and *ABC: An Alphabet Book*. The contents of the two have since been parceled out to at least six other Platt and Munk titles in both cloth and board editions at $1 or $1.50 a book. None of these cheap, shorter books could have been produced at their low prices had not the photographic contents been drawn, with no additional cost, from the earlier, more expensive books. They are good value, and good value is the yardstick that replaces literary merit in the merchandise-book field.

"I don't think a mass-market book has to be junk," Arthur Bell, writer and ex-publicist of children's books at Random House, has said, touching on the sore spot of those in the field. Despite soaring sales and shelf space in nearly every home that boasts both a roof and a child, merchandise books remain orphans— passed over by reviewers, unrewarded by annual merit medals or wide library sales, and, in the publishing world itself, denied shelter under the comforting protective mantle of Literature. "Most of America doesn't know what *The Saturday Review* is talking about," said one long-time editor in the merchandise field, "and yet all the reviewing media continue to cover only those terribly precious juvenile titles from the prestige houses—the ones that sell 4,000 copies—and ignore the books millions of children are reading." (Though millions of merchandise books are certainly sold and undoubtedly looked at with regularity by young children, there is some question as to how many are actually read.)

Certainly, so far as production is concerned, it would be a mistake to think of mass-market books as inferior. Their undeniable superiorities, in fact, are mostly related to production and price advantages. Because printing costs can be spread over so many more books sold, the merchandise publisher can afford to be lavish in the use of four-color illustration, even color photography. Thus, a large-format, 64-page mass-market book can be center-stitched (a more expensive binding than a glued one) and chock-full of color, and can sell for $1.95, while a trade-book publisher is lucky if he can bring out a much smaller-sized, 32-page book in four colors for $3.50 or $4.

Like Dr. Seuss's Cat in the Hat, the merchandise publisher can also create spectacular effects. Washable covers, spiral bindings, board pages and even moving parts prove no obstacle—so long as the ultimate sales figures justify the cost. "We're the ones who invent new formats and are always trying different ways of making information palatable and fun," one editor says with pride. Surely one of the most remarkable examples of production virtuosity on the current scene is Random House's growing line of pop-up books. Beautifully engineered by Paul Taylor of Graphics International so that almost every page provides some animation surprise, the actual work is done, generally two artists to a book, by Hallmark greeting-card illustrators. The books are then manufactured either in Japan or Singapore, where labor for such elaborate production work is still relatively cheap. In no way personal efforts, the books are the acme of imaginative assembly-line products.

Their genesis is an interesting one as well, because the first Random pop-up—Bennett Cerf's *Pop-Up Riddles* at $1.95—was produced as a Maxwell House Coffee premium promotion in 1965. The initial print order of 50,000, thought to be somewhat optimistic, sold out immediately, and Random was quick to see it had a viable merchandise book. Had Maxwell House not been there to share the risk of an expensive new venture, virtually guaranteeing bulk sales, Random would probably not have embarked on so elaborate and chancy a product. By the fall of 1969, Random was issuing eleven new pop-up titles in one season, two of them in a new science series where a genuine attempt was made to move out of the amusement and magical-theater aspects of the pop-up to provide graphic instruction in basic scientific principles. While pop-ups may be to literature what Broadway musical comedy is to Ibsen, every child ought to experience at least one of these seductive productions. (*The Night Before Christmas* at $1.95 is probably the most magical of them all.)

Special commercial tie-ins are by no means a brand-new development. Grosset has produced a number of Santa Mouse books in cooperation with J. C. Penney and recently produced a thoroughly expendable question-and-answer book using the justly famed illustrations created by Susan Perl for Health-Tex advertisements. Nor is the production move to the Orient a Random House innovation. Both Grosset's 3-D puppet storybooks and Platt and Munk's fairy-tale "action books" (the characters gyrate) are produced in Japan and Hong Kong after artwork and text are first synchronized in New York.

It is with the mention of texts that the Achilles heel of merchandise publishing is discovered, for, more often than not, words get last consideration. This is not surprising, given the priority that both the bulk buyers and the publishers assign to packaging. "It's impossible to pay royalty on both art and text in a 64-page book that sells for $1.95 or even $2.95," one editor explains. "We could not sell at the prices we do if we did." While well-known artists are often able to make some royalty arrangement with the merchandise publisher, the house itself invariably retains the copyright on art as well as text and is free to re-use the material over the years as it sees fit. Writers, almost without exception, are commissioned to provide a given number of words on an already prescribed subject (often a rewrite of someone else's text), usually within a definite format and at a prearranged flat rate. The work such a writer does may be perfectly creditable, even first-rate for what it is, but it is seldom work from the heart. Often texts are done within the house by a junior editor eager to augment her pay check. More and more frequently (as is the case in trade-book juveniles as well) an illustrator who is firmly established begins to provide his own texts as a means not only of making more money on each book but of gaining greater freedom to draw to his own specifications. Occasionally, if an editor thinks he has a potential long-term best-seller, he will pay a generous flat rate to a better-than-average writer for a text that is actually meant to be read with care. In one such case, an editor with a gift for conjuring up free-floating titles while shaving or falling asleep at night came up with *The Curiosity Book*. It was one of those perfect titles merchandise editors dream of: though new, it had a familiar, cozy ring to it and an unmistakable air of quality. It roused visions of Dickens and Merrie England; and, once you heard it, you were likely to remember it. A simple question-and-answer book seemed to fit it best, so the editor offered prime free-lance rates—but no royalties—to a competent writer and illustrator to provide the innards for his disembodied title. The book, well into a second printing of 25,000, was doing fine a year after publication.

Occasionally, of course, genius will out and a product hardheadedly devised for the mass market proves so lastingly popular that the author-illustrator becomes more important than the product he has helped to produce. Such was the case with Richard Scarry, whose lively and individualized little animals had been appearing in Golden books of varied format for more than a dozen years before his first Golden giant encyclopedia—*The Best Word Book Ever*—became a best-seller in 1963. Crammed full of small animals totally absorbed in the objects and activities of daily life, it continues to sell remarkably well. Though Mrs. Miller has said that "the one thing merchandise books cannot do is provide just the right book for Suzy"—meaning that books which seek a common denominator for multitudes of children cannot hope to appeal to the individuality of any given one—Richard Scarry has managed to get around this problem by covering all contingencies in his books. When Scarry depicts houses, foods, trucks, boats, etc., he provides so many specific varieties within the general category that he usually manages to hit the very truck, house or boat that speaks volumes to any given small viewer. This probably explains why so many young children will pore over his busy, narrative illustrations, by themselves, for unnaturally long periods of time. Scarry's more recent volumes, *What Do People Do All Day?* and *Great Big Schoolhouse,* employ the same winning encyclopedic approach, but they are now done under the Random House imprint with Scarry receiving standard trade-book royalties and his work copyrighted in his own name. That his loss was sorely felt at Golden can be surmised by the number of look-like-Scarry books the house has published since he left, as well as a national TV advertising campaign they undertook in 1969 to tout the older Scarry titles Golden owned. In fact, Golden's continued success with that author-artist's earlier work may keep his name firmly associated with that publisher in the public's mind. *The*

THINGS WE DO

There are many things
that we can do. And there
are some things we cannot do.
What is one thing we can't do?
Look and see.

dig

blow

build

break

sleep

awaken

walk

run

stand

sit

read

watch

draw and write

RICHARD SCARRY *The Best Word Book Ever*

Best Mother Goose Ever, put out by Golden late in 1970, is a case in point. The inside material comes from work done by Scarry for Golden in 1964. Yet the artist was persuaded to provide a new cover—copyrighted in his name in 1970—for the repackaging of his earlier work.

"You spend your money on the art and let the text follow" is the general rule, but this is not to say that certain editors aren't particularly conscientious about words. As Mrs. Miller pointed out, "If I kept one bad thing out of a Golden book that a million kids were going to see, it was an awesome exercise of editorial power."

One of the books in which Mrs. Miller exercised this power was a Golden Shape title, *The Sign Book,* in which loose usage in a first edition troubled her enough to insist that the text be rewritten for a second. Where in the original edition the text under a large SCHOOL CROSSING sign ran: "A school crossing sign and a zebra (white lines on the pavement) are both safe places to cross the street," Mrs. Miller felt the sentence was criminally vague ("as if there's ever really a safe place to cross a city street") and, in its specialized use of the word "zebra," confusingly esoteric. The second printing finds her entirely literal—but also strictly correct—rewrite: "The SCHOOL CROSSING sign shows boys and girls where to cross the street." In another instance Mrs. Miller showed herself to be a sounder psychologist than the original writer. Accompanying a picture of a man with green paint putting the finishing touches on a park bench, the original text ran: "Everywhere we look there are signs. Don't sit down where it says WET PAINT." Sensing a challenging invitation to disaster here, Mrs. Miller, a mother herself, altered the second edition's text to read: "There are signs everywhere. No one will sit down where it says WET PAINT."

The boundaries between merchandise and trade-book juveniles are not always clear-cut. There is a broad twilight zone where the two collide and even merge. The merchandise publisher frequently offers handy anthologies of fairy tales, Aesop's Fables, juvenile fiction in the public domain and children's poetry in tasteful, even commendable editions. In recent years Grosset has used Gyo Fujikawa to provide lush and, on the whole, sensitive illustrations for a *Child's Book of Poems,* a *Mother Goose* and *A Child's Garden of Verses*. The Provensens have illustrated several cheerful potpourris for Golden, and, thanks to the merchandise houses, one can still afford to bring a convalescing child a new book with every trip to the market.

While the thread binding them to children's literature may often be tenuous, merchandise books serve a number of positive ends. Just as Seventh Avenue has made it possible for large numbers of women to look stylish on small budgets, so merchandise publishing brings an awareness of books to countless children who never set foot in a library. Whatever one may think of many of the texts, the books' design is often excellent and the illustrations are engaging, tasteful and, on occasion, first-rate. For a child whose only extended exposure to books is through school texts or the comics, these merchandise products provide portals to the possibility of reading pleasure. One safe generalization about merchandise books is that they stick close to the common experiences and interests of childhood. No child is ever likely to be intimidated by the subject matter of a merchandise book, and few parents will be stopped by their prices. They are not investments to be protected and handled only with clean hands in the presence of a responsible adult. From a child's point of view, they probably help to give reading a good name.

There is the possibility that as merchandise publishers grow bigger and bigger—and they do with each passing year—their products will have less and less individual flavor and a higher corporate gloss. Golden has bought out several of its smaller competitors, such as Whitman; Platt and Munk in 1968 became a subsidiary of Questor Corporation; and Grosset is now part of the National General conglomerate. With the constant pressure for novelty, the business of verbal communication may recede further and further into the background. What can follow 3-D storybooks, pop-ups supreme, books that double as blocks, and others with magnetic pages? It is possible that some publisher will eventually take the mordant remark of one British author of juveniles as a challenge: "Kids like bangs. What about a book that explodes?"

9: *A Series Is a Series Is a Series*

CHILDREN who like to read, whatever their age, frequently succumb to the seductive charm of books in series. As comfortable as old shoes, as restful as sitting on the front porch listening to an endless flow of neighborhood gossip, as endearing as close friends of whose faults one is only too well aware, they can always be relied upon for hours of pleasurable company and at times much more besides. Like the vacationer who returns to a beloved summer house year after year, the addicted reader opens book three or four or eleven in a given series and is thoroughly at home in the locale—its by now familiar native characters, the verbal shrubbery and the narrative floorboards that occasionally creak.

Many a single tale may be more meritorious or memorable, but children very early become aware of the difference between a story, with its finite and separate existence in print, and real life as it is daily lived. Books in series, however, blur that distinction. They are like a constantly open window to lives in progress other than one's own. Often set in large families with multiple

heroes and heroines, they tell of children who encounter life situations and experiences different from the reader's. Usually, there
will be at least one character with whom the reading child can
deeply identify, a boy or girl of similar temperament or age, and
then that fortunate reader—by the most marvelous feat of magic
of which books in series are capable—is able to live simultaneously
his own life and another, freer, sadder, happier, richer, poorer or
simply different from his own.

I can still recall the shock of recognition in discovering Jo,
an alter self, in the pages of Louisa May Alcott's *Little Women:*

> Jo immediately sat up, put her hands in her pockets and began
> to whistle.
> "Don't, Jo; it's so boyish!"
> "That's why I do it!"

Books in series do much to establish in children the healthy
understanding that life is not a perfectly rounded tale, but rather
an endless string of adventures and misadventures. Today's defeat may be the foundation for next year's triumph. Series also
do much to indicate the slow process of growth in human understanding, judgment and character. In Kate Douglas Wiggin's
Rebecca of Sunnybrook Farm, the heroine worships her handsome, gifted father. Her hard-working mother, who is busy having babies, sewing and keeping the household together, seems drab
to her by comparison. At the end of *New Chronicles of Rebecca,*
however, she has begun to understand her mother's quiet virtues
and at what cost to others her father's charm and glamour were
maintained. She remembers an occasion on which her father
chided his wife for not caring more about her appearance. (At the

time, she was carefully tying his tie so that he could leave for a "sociable.")

Mother had finished the tie, and her hands dropped suddenly. I looked at her eyes and mouth while she looked at father and in a minute I was ever so old with a grown-up ache in my heart. . . . Father was always the favorite when we were little, he was so interesting, and I wonder sometimes if we don't remember interesting people longer and better than we do those who are just good and patient. If so, it seems very cruel.

The best series are primers of life. Often, they will provide a child with a first relationship in depth outside the confines of his own immediate family circle. In so doing, they perhaps serve the genre's richest purpose. Laura Ingalls Wilder's eight books about life on the American frontier one hundred years ago, beginning with *Little House in the Big Woods,* give a living sense of the nation's pioneering past, of the quality of family life then and of how it felt to be part of the wagon trains moving westward. Sydney Taylor's three *All-of-a-Kind Family* sagas provide the vicarious experience of growing up the offspring of Jewish immigrants in turn-of-the-century New York. When children are asked which of the All-of-a-Kind books is their favorite, it is usually the first that is mentioned. In that volume, the family struggles hardest and its way of life on the Lower East Side seems most exotic to children today. Once the All-of-a-Kind Family moves uptown to the Bronx, it loses much of its earlier unique quality, becoming rather like next-door neighbors. Children from seven to eleven no longer look for mirrors of their lives in books but rather for windows on the wider world. Elizabeth Enright's trio of tales about

GARTH WILLIAMS *Little House in the Big Woods*

the four Melendy children (*The Saturdays, The Four-Story Mistake* and *Then There Were Five*) concerns a family in which the mother dies—a cataclysm unthinkable to most children in their waking lives—and how the Melendys manage to fill the void. Though almost no one today reads Eleanor Porter's *Pollyanna* books, they start out with an eleven-year-old orphan coming to live with a dutiful spinster aunt who refuses to love her "just because I happened to have a sister who was silly enough to marry and bring unnecessary children into the world." Such series, more than individual stories, will often expand the child's vision of life's possibilities both for good and for evil, of the remarkable versatility and resiliency of the human spirit in the face of adversity, and of life's peculiar long-term justice, a function of effort, time and chance playing upon human character. Just as the child's first and most meaningful teacher in life is his own family, so many series—taking place as they do within a family context—provide rich learning experiences beyond the limits of the child's own household horizons.

For this same seven-to-eleven age group, there is also a different sort of series which plucks the child from his own time and place and sets him down in other, imagined worlds as convincing as his own. Mary Norton's five volumes about the tiny race of Borrowers, C. S. Lewis' seven tales of "That Place" Narnia and, more recently, Lloyd Alexander's sagas of the medieval Kingdom of Prydain strongly suggest that all lives, real or magical, have an inherent order and logic. There are lessons to be learned, responsibilities to be carried out and rules to be obeyed not only within one's own family or school but even—and sometimes especially—in fairylands. Through return visits to such sustained fantasy worlds the child begins to gain some perspective on and insight into his own world.

What most of us first think of when "series" are mentioned —whole country-library shelves of Nancy Drew and Hardy Boys mysteries, Tom Swift's adventures and the Rover Boys' rovings —comprise a pre-adolescent escape literature. Decidedly regressions so far as literary or human content are concerned, they play subtly upon the restlessness and idealism of older children, perhaps even staving off adolescent depression with their pure fantasies of the power of youth and the glory of the life of action. Lo the poor ten- and eleven-year-olds, for whom time hangs suspended between childhood and man's estate, for whom little that is meaningful seems ever to happen in the here and now. They have outgrown the best of childhood's privileges, yet have attained almost none of the prerogatives of adulthood. Their parents and assorted elders still control large areas of their lives. To their frequent lament that nothing ever happens, the authors of such popular series have their heroes and heroines move all over the globe in cars, planes, steam yachts, air gliders and submarines to solve a seemingly endless chain of mysteries and best assorted villains of all ages. Though the protagonists of these works are perennial high-school students, a permanently fixed fifteen-to-seventeen, they have no difficulty driving the air-conditioned convertibles, or commanding the ships, motorboats and planes needed to jet-propel the plot from incident to unlikely incident. They have all the mechanical symbols of power their readers lack and an almost magical mobility to roam the globe on constantly varying urgent missions.

While to adults this literature seems to be Walter Mittyism unredeemed by wit, it can, for a time, wholly absorb many children who feel they are too old to play games of make-believe themselves but are happy to lose themselves in fantasy adventures of slightly older heroes and heroines that are disguised as true-life documentaries. Each action-packed adventure, in any case, rests on the bedrock of conventional practicality and sensible rules of day-to-day behavior which surely would rate general grownup approval. Though the Hardy boys and Nancy Drew encounter assorted wicked villains who behave bizarrely, they themselves always act with commendable decorum, paragons of well-brought-up young citizenry. Joe and Frank Hardy may be in hot pursuit of an elusive assailant, but they stop their convertible for all red lights and give chase "without breaking the speed limit." Nancy Drew, aroused from slumber by a mysterious intruder, jumps out of bed, but does not give chase before "putting on robe and slippers." When school chums of the Hardys join them in an afternoon's sleuthing, they do not forget at its end "to phone their families that they were all right." Moving into a client's house to help Nancy Drew solve a particularly puzzling case, her two girl friends Bess and George do not fail "to dust their rooms" like good guests, and no matter how pressing her detective work, Nancy Drew herself generally manages to take Sunday dinner at home and attend church with her lawyer father. Beneath the façade of exotic adventure, these stories are practical handbooks for getting along successfully in the workaday world. "Let's do our searching systematically," Frank Hardy suggests to his brother at the start of *The Secret of Pirates Hill*, and his approach to the boys' current problem would wholly satisfy any junior-high-school teacher of logic. Just as everything in children's first picture books suggests an ordered, comprehensible universe, so, too, these mystery adventures always yield ultimately to the heroes' or heroines' applied intelligence. The constantly repeated message that the forthcoming mysteries of adult life are manageable, using one's own good sense, is part of these books' perennial appeal.

The fact that series' adventures are usually set in reasonably realistic locales heightens the reader's feeling that he is learning about life in the wider world. In the preface to *The Rover Boys at School* (1899), Edward Stratemeyer wrote:

> My Dear Boys: *The Rover Boys at School* has been written so that those of you who have never put in a term or more at an American military academy for boys may gain some insight into the workings of such an institution.

Victor Appleton noted of his *Tom Swift* adventures, "It is the purpose of these spirited tales to convey in a realistic way the wonderful advances in land and sea locomotion." And in recent years, each new adventure of the Hardy Boys or Nancy Drew has introduced a minimal amount of information about some particular hobby or vocation. Thus, in *The Clue of the Tapping Heels,* a Nancy Drew mystery, a major character is a breeder of Persian cats and the reader gets a vague sense of the work entailed in their care, feeding, showing and sale. In *The Secret of Pirates Hill,* the Hardy Boys become involved in the unearthing of a centuries-old Spanish cannon, a demiculvern by classification, and learn something of the weapon's use, range and unique appearance. But such authentic details of setting and incident are surely simply frosting to the central glorification of youthful competence, the message that boys and girls are fully capable of coping and of doing something that counts.

From *The Bobbsey Twins at the Ice Carnival* comes one formulation of the prevailing message:

As Bert stumbled through the heat and smoke he thought of other adventures when he had had to convince grownups that he was doing a worthwhile thing and not just getting in their way. They never gave a fellow credit for having common sense, he thought!

Of what importance is it that the books are written in a wooden prose rife with clichés? "Tom pluckily overcame all obstacles." . . . " 'Nan Bobbsey! What a pleasant surprise!' the wealthy woman greeted her." . . . The children who read them never stop to notice that Nancy Drew's eyes are invariably "sparkling" as she laughs "merrily," nor do they seem to mind the inordinate amount of gasping and gulping the characters do during crises. Just as Jo daydreams in *Little Women,* "I want to do something splendid . . . something heroic and wonderful that won't be forgotten after I'm dead," so too the readers of Dave Dawson's or Nancy Drew's mock-adult escapades long for conquests beyond the gates of childhood.

The resolution of any single adventure is of negligible interest. It is the excitement of the narrative journey which counts. For 213 pages of *The Secret of Pirates Hill,* the Hardy Boys are on the trail of nebulous treasure. Though they finally unearth it on the closing page, the reader never learns of what it consists or what value it may have. Rather, the reward lies in discovering that the Hardys' next adventure will be *The Ghost at Skeleton Rock,* still another open door to escape from the drab realities of childhood's twilight.

In *Eight Cousins,* Louisa May Alcott objected to such adventure series as her contemporary Oliver Optic was then churning out, precisely on the grounds of their falsity to life, complaining:

"I am not satisfied with these *optical delusions,* as I call them. Now, I put it to you, boys, is it natural for lads from fifteen to eighteen to command ships, defeat pirates, outwit smugglers, and so cover themselves with glory, that Admiral Farragut invites them to dinner, saying: 'Noble boy, you are an honor to your country!' "

Most readers of similar series today, once the latest volume is closed, are probably as aware of their unlikelihood as was Miss Alcott. Yet it is part of the books' charm. As Optic (William T. Adams) himself put it at the height of a career which produced more than a hundred books in series, "Do not keep young minds always on the high pressure system of instruction." Children, like adults, tire of doing and reading things because they are worthwhile and will benefit them. These series represent a final stage of childhood reading: playing at being grownup before one begins to take the matter seriously as a teenager. If many children are all too eager to lose themselves in their assorted mysteries and secrets, treasure hunts and searches for giants, perhaps it is a form of distraction from the mysteries of grownup sexuality which will shortly confront them.

There is a curious similarity that seems to run through a majority of books in series regardless of their age level or quality: The families of most of the heroes and heroines have only one parent. Elsie Dinsmore, that paragon of Victorian virtues and the heroine of Martha Finley's interminable series of adventures from infancy to grandmotherhood, tells the reader: "Since my own dear mama has gone to heaven, papa is enough for me." In Victor Appleton's Tom Swift books, "Father and son lived in a fine house . . . and Mrs. Swift being dead, the two were well looked after by Mrs. Baggert their housekeeper.'' The mother of the Rover Boys has ''died of a fever'' when Dick Rover, the eldest brother, was ten, before the series opens. The father of *The Five Little Peppers* has also died off stage, ''when Phronsie was a baby.'' Carolyn Keene's Nancy Drew lives alone with her father and their housekeeper, Hannah Gruen. Eleanor Estes' *The Moffats* are fatherless, for Papa ''died when Rufus was just a tiny baby''; and Elizabeth Enright says of the Melendy children in *The Saturdays,* ''It was sad that they had no mother, but they did have Father and he could not have been improved upon as a parent.'' As for E. Nesbit's Bastable children, the reader quickly learns:

We are the Bastables. There are six of us beside Father. Our mother is dead, and if you think we don't care because I don't tell you much about her, you only show that you do not understand people at all.

Even where both parents are alive, they are seldom both present. In *Little Women,* the father of the family is off serving with the Union troops in the Civil War. And the Walker children in Arthur Ransome's *Swallows and Amazons* and subsequent books have a seafaring father who is generally on duty with the Royal Navy in far-off places.

This family imbalance does several things, both for the children within the tales and for those outside who read rapt of their lives. For the heroes and heroines of the tales, the absence of a mother or a father generally means deprivations of various sorts. ''Mrs. Pepper had had hard work to scrape together money enough to put bread into her children's mouths, and to pay the rent of the little brown house.'' The five children often eat ''cold potatoes for their breakfast'' and the youngest of them, Phronsie, says wistfully, ''Sometime, we're going to be *awful* rich.'' Almost any child reading the first book of their adventures already feels rich by comparison. '' 'It's so dreadful to be poor!' sighed Meg'' begins the second sentence of *Little Women*. The Moffats' mother works long hours as ''the finest dressmaker in the town of Cranbury'' to keep her family in their wonderful yellow house. And the Bastable children throughout *The Treasure Seekers* devote their energies to restoring ''the fallen fortunes of our house.'' Many children in series lack the things their well-fed readers have come to take for granted, or even to regard as burdens more than privileges. The Bastable children cannot go to school until their father is solvent again; the Peppers too are at home by necessity, though their mother thinks constantly of ways to help them get an education. The children who read these books are given new yard-sticks by which to measure the quality of their own existences. The child who has grumbled because she could not get a new dress for a birthday party is chastened by the suffering of proud Meg in *Little Women* who, on a visit to rich friends near Boston, must wear an old, limp, countrified party dress to a sophisticated gathering of her peers. Such series serve subtle portions of much the same lesson Mrs. March tries to impart in an improvised parable to the Little Women:

''Once upon a time, there were four girls, who had enough to eat and drink and wear, a good many comforts and pleas-ures, kind friends and parents, who loved them dearly, and yet they were not contented.'' (Here the listeners stole sly looks at one another, and began to sew diligently.) ''These girls were anxious to be good, and made many excellent resolutions; but they did not keep them very well, and were constantly saying, 'If we only had this,' or 'If we could only do that,' quite forgetting how much they already had, and how many pleasant things they actually could do. . . .''

But if family circumstances require sacrifices and the assumption of more adult responsibilities—like taking jobs and keeping house—by children in series, they also give them a great deal more time on their own to discover abilities and to test themselves in a variety of life situations without parental scrutiny or well-meaning interference. In most of the series books, the children suffer a benign neglect. The remaining parent is so preoccupied with responsibilities—the burden of caring for a large family, the necessity to earn money—that he or she cannot focus full attention on the children. As Oswald, who speaks for the Bastables, relates:

> Father sat in the armchair. It was jolly. He doesn't often come and talk to us now. He has to spend all his time thinking about his business.

Thus, the children in the books have a much freer rein than most of the children who read about them. Part of the lasting appeal of such series lies in the fact that they secretly fulfill the longing of all children for more freedom to test their own competence, a freedom to learn by trial and error, to make unobserved mistakes as well as to succeed. What would it be like to have no parents just for a little while? The child finds out in Laura Ingalls Wilder's *Farmer Boy* when the four Wilder children must keep house by themselves for a whole week. Scarcely is the parental buggy out of sight when the children assume their responsibilities:

"What'll we do first?"

"We'll do the dishes and make the beds and sweep," Eliza Jane said.

"I'll tell you," Royal said, "let's make ice cream!"

And so begins a week of feasting and pleasure. The children make ice cream, candy, cake and sit in the forbidden parlor "like company." What does it matter that they leave a week's chores till the very last day if self-discipline miraculously gets all the weeding, dusting, mopping and churning done? It is not that children are irresponsible; their priorities are simply different.

And what reader does not envy the motherless Bastables just a little bit for their leisurely afternoons of play:

Just then Pincher [their dog] jumped up and knocked over the painting-water. He is a very careless dog. I wonder why painting-water is always such an ugly colour. Dora ran for a duster to wipe it up, and H.O. dropped drops of the water on his hands and said he had got the plague. So we played at the plague for a bit, and I was an Arab physician with a bath-towel turban, and cured the plague with magic acid-drops.

Necessity also seems to make the remaining parent in series books more reasonable. Though Mr. Melendy in *The Saturdays* gives his children the traditional warning "Don't talk to strangers" as they leave on their solo trips into downtown Manhattan, he tempers the advice with a sensible amendment: "Unless you know by looking at them that they're kind people, and even then

141

think twice." The Walker children's absent father in *Swallows and Amazons*, when petitioned by wire to permit his offspring to take an extended sailing trip by themselves, cables his marvelously logical and terse approval: BETTER DROWNED THAN DUFFERS IF NOT DUFFERS WON'T DROWN. Most young readers are enchanted by this message, since it is common knowledge that most real-life parents would rather their children be duffers than drown.

On their own so much, the children in series do occasionally steal, lie and deceive—often with the noblest motives—but the lessons they learn from life are far more eloquent than parental warnings and sermonizing. When the Bastables purposely set their dog on Lord Tottenham, hoping to restore the family fortunes via the rescue of "an old gentleman from deadly peril," they are ignominiously found out. Their punishment lies in facing up to the irresponsibility of their plan:

> "A very nice way to make your fortune—by deceit and trickery. I have a horror of dogs. If I'd been a weak man, the shock might have killed me. What do you think of yourselves, eh?"
>
> We were all crying except Oswald, and the others say he was; and Lord Tottenham went on—
>
> "Well, well, I see you're sorry. Let this be a lesson to you; and we'll say no more about it. . . . Always remember never to do a dishonourable thing, for money or for anything else in the world."

Books in series are perhaps best loved by children because they comprise declarations of independence from adult-imposed standards and judgments. Most of their authors write authoritatively from the child's point of view. As William Taylor Adams confessed in the preface to one of his many series tales: "The author of the following story pleads guilty to being more than half a boy himself . . . he has no difficulty in stepping back over the weary waste of years. . . ." He was not alone in the gift. When Elizabeth Enright in *The Saturdays* has the ten-year-old Miranda tell of her afternoon tea with music in a genteel New York hotel, the room comes alive as only a child would see it with the observation: "All the musicians looked about 50 years old. . . ." And E. Nesbit makes quite clear to her readers whose side she is on at the start of *Five Children and It:*

> Now that I have begun to tell you about the place, I feel that I could go on and make this into a most interesting story about all the ordinary things that the children did—just the kind of things you do yourself, you know . . . and when I told about the children's being tiresome, as you are sometimes, your aunts would perhaps write in the margin of the story with a pencil, "How true!" or "How like life!" and you would see it and very likely be annoyed. So I will only tell you the really astonishing things that happened, and you may leave the book about quite safely, for no aunts or uncles either are likely to write "How true!" on the edge of the story.

In books in series, it is a safe generalization that children observe, enjoy and learn from the successes and failures of their peers.

An additional curious feature of books in series is that their authors seldom embarked upon them entirely from the heart. It took a persuasive publisher to convince Louisa May Alcott that she should even attempt a story for girls based on her own experiences. "I don't enjoy this sort of thing," she complained.

"Never liked girls or knew many except my sisters, but our queer plays and experiences may prove interesting, though I doubt it." Spurred on, however, by what she called "the inspiration of necessity"—she was the chief support of the Alcott family—she turned out *Little Women,* which, much to both publisher's and author's surprise, became an immediate hit. Louisa went on to its sequel, *Good Wives* (incorporated into modern U.S. editions of *Little Women*), more cheerfully, noting that "A little success is so inspiring." E. Nesbit's was a similar route. Under economic pressure and at the behest of the editor of the *Girls' Own Paper,* she attempted to provide reminiscences of her school days. She dreamed of being a poet or a serious novelist for adults (a dream also harbored by Horatio Alger), but, much like the mother in her own *The Railway Children* who is her family's only source of income, she spent "almost all day shut up in her upstairs room, writing, writing, writing"; and out of "the happy memories of that golden time"—her own childhood—she produced two beloved children's series.

The creators of *Elsie Dinsmore* and *The Rover Boys,* in prefaces to later works in these series, expressed surprise bordering on resignation that their stories had continued over so long a period. And the number of series which are offered under pseudonyms or syndicated names—Henry Castlemon, Oliver Optic, Margaret Sidney, Arthur Winfield, Carolyn Keene, etc.—suggest that their authors, individually or collectively, may not have considered their work of sufficient substance to claim in their own names. Yet the very fact that many authors of series seem to take their work with a grain of salt accounts for part of the genre's special flavor. Just as a traveler will strike up a casual friendship on board ship, often revealing more about himself than he has to

dear friends at home simply because it doesn't seem to matter—
he's unlikely to see the person again—so too the series' writer
relaxes in a way that an author bent on producing a literary
masterpiece never can. As he rambles on, thinking it does not matter on a cosmic plane, he occasionally reveals more of himself and
the truth of given situations than he ever imagined. And his tone,
often more confidential and enticing than that employed in more
literary works, flatters his young audience. One can usually tell
the book that is part of a series, though E. Nesbit's *The Railway Children* is a genuine disappointment because it ought to be
and isn't.

When a series is undistinguished—the Bobbsey Twins, Nancy
Drew, or the Hardy Boys—it is simply a banal, though assuredly
benign form of escape from the confines of self. But when one is
good, as are the tales of E. Nesbit, Arthur Ransome, and Laura
Ingalls Wilder, it is often very very good and, like other best
friends made in childhood, will never be entirely forgotten.

10: *Mechanics of Survival: Why Publish? Who Judges?*

MANY too many books are published," a forthright English juvenile editor said to her American counterpart recently, stating a simple, unarguable truth that, in part, has been the result of unparalleled technical virtuosity in the service of nearly universal literacy during an extended period of prosperity. In addition, in the United States, increased public concern about early learning and curriculum-enrichment materials for the public schools has brought the lure of city, state and federal funds into an already healthy juvenile book-buying market. During the 1950s and '60s the list of American publishers with children's-book departments has lengthened steadily, with more than fifty providing titles under their own imprints by the spring of 1970.

If, indeed, the present quarter century—1950 to 1975—retains its contemporary reputation as a golden age of children's literature, its hallmark is likely to be the incredible number of books available rather than the superior quality of the outstanding few. In any given season, the prospective buyer can have his pick of a dozen gifted illustrators' improvisations on nursery rhymes or traditional tales. New alphabet and counting books replace the old almost before a bookstore clerk has had a chance to become familiar with the parting season's promising titles; and a single popular artist or author has been known to have as many as three titles appear in one season, all for the same age group and each under the imprint of a different publishing house. Five years ago, two superior versions of *The Twelve Dancing Princesses* came out simultaneously, one illustrated by Uri Shulevitz based on a new translation from the Brothers Grimm, the other a rendition of a French telling of the tale with artwork by Adrienne Adams. More recently, both Ed Emberley and Peter Spier, gifted graphic interpreters, provided individual views of the fall of London Bridge at the same time, and in the spring of 1970 two new editions of *Androcles and the Lion* appeared, one done by the veteran illustrator Paul Galdone, the other by Janusz Grabianski. It is a rare season, too, which does not have at least one new picture-book variation on the Noah's Ark theme, a simple tale about a child's wonder at the first snowfall, or a wisp of a romance about walking in the rain with new boots and one's very own umbrella. For grownups who have no close contact with particular children, this seemingly endless repetition of the same simple themes is one of the enigmas of the juvenile-book genre. It is easy to forget that adult works, and life as well, are repetitive —variations on more complex patterns and themes.

While this embarrassment of riches is surely a delight to the well-to-do parent browsing in a well-stocked bookstore, its existence cannot be credited to the buying power of individuals. At an average price of $4 for a four-color picture book, and with production costs climbing as each publishing season passes, there are not many people who can afford to buy children's books, except for special occasions. Schools and libraries, the mainstays of juvenile publishing, account for 80 to 85 percent of the sales of children's books published today. With a clientele of young learners, listeners and readers in the millions, and with books replaced at an annual rate exceeding 15 percent in some large metropolitan public libraries, educators and librarians are insatiable purchasers of children's books. Why not order copies of two different versions of a Grimm tale, three new interpretations of *Little Red Riding Hood,* and four Mother Goose collections of varying size and shape? Some children may enjoy Raymond Briggs's slapstick drolleries, but others surely will opt for Marguerite de Angeli's lyricism.

Yet, with up to 3,000 new books appearing annually to compete in this thriving market, it is legitimate to wonder how so many publishers are able to find a continuous flow of quality manuscripts to fill each season's lists. The answer, of course, is that often they do not; and one of the best and clearest explanations as to why they continue to publish less than superior fare for a seemingly oversupplied book market has come from Atheneum's editor of children's books, Jean Karl, in a *Horn Book* piece on the subject of editing books for children. "Few books are excellent," she readily acknowledged. "Not every book I have published is a book I would consider excellent. This is true for many reasons. Sometimes, an editor takes a first book that shows promise because she thinks better books will follow from the author. Sometimes an editor takes a book that is good, not excellent, because the book has qualities that will fill an important need in an area where excellence is hard to find. . . . Children demand up-to-date information and with current demands to be met publishers can seldom wait the length of time necessary to find and publish a book of real excellence.''

Occasionally, this desire on the part of alert publishers to provide ''up-to-date information'' on a topic currently in vogue will result in three or four books on the same subject appearing at once, none of them of any special distinction. Yet each of them will sell reasonably well simply because other sources on the subject are nonexistent, or hopelessly dated, and both schools and libraries are eager to keep their collections of informational books contemporaneous with developments.

Institutional sales are generally far more vital to the success of a children's title than an adult one. Some juvenile departments will cautiously consult with veteran librarians and educators before finally formulating a proposed new series, and more than one juvenile editor has been known to submit a manuscript about which there was some reservation to a librarian reader of the editor's choice for another professional opinion. Since school and library sales generally mean the difference between a profit and loss on most titles, no experienced editor lightly dismisses the thought of the institutional market from her judgments. Yet, the complaint that far too much power over what is published for and read by children lies with librarians is often heard and bears close examination.

''They [children's books] have to be *nice*,'' a nameless editor explained to Eleanor Cameron for a 1966 *Horn Book* piece. ''All librarians want kids' books to be nice.'' Is the assessment just? It is only fair to note that librarians alone, aside from the more dedicated authors, artists and publishers who produce them, have a lifelong professional interest in children's books. When his or her children grow up, a parent no longer dutifully follows the

Sunday *Times* or *Chicago Tribune* reviews of new juvenile
titles. Children themselves, quick to outgrow their tastes of the
moment, devour particular stories one year, yet will have lost all
interest in a given genre by the next. Even the perceptive critic
for the newspapers is unlikely to make a long-time career of reviewing children's books; it is usually an occasional pastime, with
the critic interested in a particular kind of book. The librarian's
unquestionable value as judge is that he or she can honestly claim
to know the tastes of a wide variety of children on a thoroughly
workaday and practical level over a continuous and extended
period of time. In such a context, the recent review of a book
titled *An Album of Black Americans in the Armed Forces,* which
the American Library Association's *Booklist* judged a work "of
great browsing interest to non-reading Negro boys 6–9," makes
perfect sense and has use, at least to other librarians. In part, it

150

is the librarian's role to deal with thousands of books as commodities in a practical, businesslike context. The stock that will move is good. By the same token, because the librarian orders books in quantity and must have in mind the tastes of all sorts of children, a meritorious work that will appeal to only a handful of her clientele during its library-shelf career is also likely to be ordered and judiciously recommended.

A sore point among many juvenile editors, authors and artists has long been the generally low quality of the reviews which appear in the librarians' professional journals and their undue power to make or break a given title. Both the innovative young editor who decides to publish a thoroughly off-beat work and his more conservative colleague who sticks with the tried and true must hope for good reviews in *School Library Journal* and the ALA *Booklist,* the two most influential professional publications to reach children's librarians. An unfavorable review in either diminishes a book's sales potential, and negative reviews in both can spell disaster. Surely to the non-librarian reader scanning the brief reviews in either of these publications, their level seems distressingly pedestrian, even oblivious to many a book's true quality. Particularly with books for younger children, extra points seem often to go to those works which raise no possibilities for troubled thoughts. In the spring of 1970, a droll confection entitled *The Elephant and the Bad Baby* by Elfrida Vipont was judged too stimulating for naptime fare, and even Maurice Sendak's *Where the Wild Things Are,* though it ultimately received the Caldecott Medal from librarians, was greeted with grave reservations in at least one journal because of the artist's wholehearted portrayal of the monsters of his hero Max's fantasy life. Most curious, perhaps, in these professional-journal reviews is the uniform lack of intelligent attention to the quality of illustration in an age when illustration has reached such heights both in conception and in execution. There are repeated references to artwork as "clever" or "cartoonlike." The noticeable repetition of certain key phrases, in fact, suggests that a list of criteria may be provided to reviewers for these journals and that few librarians stray beyond them.

That the librarians' journals provide unsatisfactory and inadequate literary judgments of children's books cannot be argued. But, as Paul Heins, the editor of *Horn Book,* observed late in 1970, "Perhaps one should distinguish, in the long run, between the two different ways of approaching children's books: (1) the criticism of these books as they concern the different kinds of people who use and work with them and (2) the literary criticism of children's literature." The librarians' journals have seldom aspired to Heins's second category, though, as one editor who feels librarians are often unjustly maligned puts it, "Probably the best and most knowledgeable literary criticism of children's books in this country today takes place behind closed doors, during library purchase-committee meetings."

The more literary and perceptively written reviews are to be found, on occasion, in *Horn Book,* the single independent journal totally devoted to children's books and their authors, and in *The New York Times Book Review* and *Book World.* These media, however—particularly the latter two—have surprisingly little influence by comparison to the library publications. While a front-page review in a *Times Book Review's* children's issue a few years back was credited with selling as many as 30,000 copies of Richard Lewis' collection of children's poetry, *Miracles,* in bookstores, this was a rare, perhaps a unique, phenomenon. Two other trade journals, *Publishers' Weekly* and *The Kirkus Reviews,* are consulted more by booksellers and jobbers. Their reviews, usually somewhat longer and more selective than the librarians', are presented with an eye toward uncovering possible bookstore best-sellers.

If there is a danger in the growing power of librarians and other institutional buyers, it lies not so much in their conservatism, real or imagined, as in the possibility that, with ever rising costs and tightened purchase budgets, publishers themselves will tend to choose the safer, less innovative works in order to minimize risk. Certainly publishers and librarians alike already look with favor on well-established authors and illustrators whose books have a history of enthusiastic reception. Even in the booming children's-book market that has prevailed over the past decade, the well-known artist or writer has often been encouraged by his editor to undertake yet another version of *Old Mother Hubbard* (though Arnold Lobel and Raymond Briggs may each have done a superior rendition of the same subject within recent memory) or some equally tried and thoroughly unadventurous work. The very familiarity of the subject helps to assure wide, long-term sales.

If there is, on the one hand, already a conspicuous tendency to overpublish the safe, the truly creative editor has thus far managed not to be unduly hampered by the economic realities and sales structure of children's-book publishing. In 1965 a new and highly original artist, Harriet Pincus, made her debut with a picture book titled *The Wedding Procession of the Rag Doll and the Broom Handle and Who Was in It*. It was an inspired choice of book for the première appearance by an illustrator of Miss Pincus' idiosyncratic and special talent. The fame of the book's author, Carl Sandburg, helped to pave the way for the work's wide notice and her deserved favorable reception. Because publishing costs are high and grow increasingly higher, the wise editor tries to protect his firm's investment in new talent by such marriages of convenience between gifted, unknown illustrators or authors and writers or artists with firmly established reputation. Thus launched, Miss Pincus had little difficulty gaining further commissions, and her most recent work, illustrations for Lore Segal's *Tell Me a Mitzi,* marks the full flowering of a major new children's-book illustrator. This last work, a highly special collaboration of wry storytelling and virtuoso pictorial improvisation, would probably not have received so elaborate and expensive a production (the four-color, large-format picture book was priced at $4.95) if Miss Pincus' career had not been so auspiciously launched and if the editor of *Mitzi* had not felt confident of the book's ability to attract wide critical notice. In this instance, the existence of librarians' buying power can be viewed as a liberating one, for it may have spurred the publisher to undertake an artistic venture whose costs could otherwise have been prohibitive. Though the reviews of the Pincus-Segal book were wholly laudatory, few took note of the book's special quality: its poetic, bittersweet grasp, both in text and pictures, of the fragile will-o'-the-wisps of adventure and misadventure that comprise the flavor of childhood. It was heralded more as slapstick comedy than as a moving literary experience in picture-book form. But most editors, authors and illustrators (of juvenile or adult books) are grateful for favorable reviews in the library journals. They scarcely hope for sensitive or pointedly intelligent ones.

There is, however, a particular form of discouragement and melancholy to which seriously committed children's authors and artists occasionally fall victim. No matter how good their work, only minimal space is allotted to the review and recognition of children's books in literary journals for the general public. The best and most perceptive critic is generally given a mixed batch of picture books or tales to review in the briefest number of words, and though most of the media that cover children's books put out occasional lists of the best of them ("the best, not of all possible books, but of the actual books published during a specified time," as Paul Heins has been careful to point out), the constant stream of new books makes even these gleanings seem exercises in futility. Editors, their authors and illustrators must continually do battle against the sea of children's books, hoping in some way to keep particularly deserving works from being lost in the deluge of ever new titles. Out of 2,300 brief evaluations of children's books printed in *School Library Journal* during 1967, the editors' annual choice of the cream of the crop was a selection of just 56 children's titles, supplemented by an additional 31 books from the adult works reviewed that year which were deemed of special interest to children.

Oddly enough, the seasoned librarian or book reviewer, like the veteran movie or TV critic, often grows mellower rather than harsher in his evaluations as time passes. Out of the stack of indifferent and truly bad work that he sees, even the middling begins to look pretty good. Little by little, he acquires an appreciation of the subtler aspects of book production which escape the general reader's notice—such as design, binding and color register —and the medium itself rather than the audience for which the particular work was intended becomes his frame of reference. Because the dedicated author or illustrator whose work is consistently superior gets little more space or appreciation than the hack, he begins to feel that he is the practitioner of a minor art form which merits no more serious recognition. Though thousands of children may finger the pages of his work with inarticulate delight, he gets little feedback from this highest form of tribute. Not even the annual Newbery and Caldecott awards or the spring Children's Book Festival's choice of prize books can make up for the routinely pedestrian level of critical attention he has received through the years from the wider world of literature.

Still deeper cause for general concern about young children's literature may ultimately lie in the fact that the four-color picture book is fast becoming a production luxury that few publishers who print in the United States can afford. As one experienced editor confessed in the fall of 1970, "We can really no longer experiment with picture books—not when it means, as our production department recently estimated, a price of $7.95 for a proposed full-color book." Also, recent cutbacks in federal funds for education have caused a noticeable tapering off in book sales. Though there has been legitimate cause to lament the superfluous production of redundant works—of flashy, outsize picture books when they were in vogue, or of basal readers in doggerel when Dr. Seuss made that genre as much a fad as the hula hoop—the prospect that gifted artists and writers will no longer be attracted to the genre, as they have been in recent years, is still more lamentable.

11: Black Is Bountiful

*Today . . . the Indian stands reborn—in a fine
clean region of his own, half way between DiMag-
gio and Christ. . . . There is certainly charm in
this tardy deification of the American primitive,
but it sometimes strikes me as a little far from
life: . . . or maybe I don't meet the right Indians.*

E. B. WHITE, *"One Man's Heart"*
(Harper's Magazine, *January 1939*)

*Sometimes people get on your nerves and they
don't mean it or nothin' but they just bother you.
Why I gotta put up with him?*

JOHN STEPTOE, Stevie
(*Harper & Row, 1969*)

NCE upon a time there was a little black boy and his
name was Little Black Sambo. He enjoyed a mild success both in England, where he was first published in
1899, and, in translation, on the Continent. His truly
remarkable success, however, came in the United
States, where for a long while he was the only little black boy to
appear as the hero of any book, for children or adults. Surprisingly, to those readers with a long-standing affection for Little
Black Sambo, he has not been made an honorary member of the
NAACP. In fact, for some twenty years now, he has been the
object of a concerted cold-shoulder campaign by that organization
and others, their aim being his exclusion from schools, libraries
and publishers' juvenile lists throughout the land. The grounds
are that Helen Bannerman, his creator, presents in her drawings
an unflattering stereotype of black people, that her names are dis-

respectful, and that her protagonists therefore are meant to be objects of ridicule rather than genuine heroes or heroines.

Somewhat old hat by now, Sambo's case is worth one last re-examination, for it takes place far enough back in literary history to be viewed dispassionately. Yet the issues it raises still cloud black-white literary horizons today. Helen Bannerman was a genteel Scottish lady, the daughter of an Episcopal clergyman and the wife of a physician who devoted his life to stamping out malaria in India. By way of preface to the authorized American edition of her work, the publisher noted of its genesis: ''Once upon a time there was an English lady in India, where black children abound and tigers are everyday affairs, who had two little girls. To amuse these little girls she used now and then to invent stories, for which, being extremely talented, she also drew and coloured the pictures.'' Little Black Sambo's ardent defenders are always quick to point out that his homeland is India. ''After all,'' they say, ''the story isn't even about Negroes.'' But if it is not, we may legitimately inquire why Mumbo, Jumbo and Little Black Sambo have such distinctly African features. Surely Mrs. Bannerman had Indians enough around her in Bombay or Madras to achieve better likenesses. The fact is, the book was conceived elsewhere.

Little Black Sambo was written not in India but in England during Mrs. Bannerman's trip home to place her two young daughters in school at Edinburgh. Feeling lonely on her return train ride to London, she wrote and illustrated *Sambo* to send as part of a letter. Why Mrs. Bannerman, sketching from memory, should depict black people as she did may well be explained by the fact that she herself had memories of a different black population. As the daughter of a clergyman who was also an Army chaplain, she had spent the impressionable years of her childhood in various parts of the British Empire. Between the ages of two and ten she had lived on Madeira, off the west coast of Africa, where black Africans were a sizable element in a mixed population. Surely the dress of her Black Jumbo is more appropriate to a black man of such a semi-tropical, cosmopolitan locale (the West Indies suggested themselves before one knew Mrs. Bannerman's history) than to a native of remotest India. And the characters' names—Black Mumbo and Black Jumbo—which bring to mind the phrase ''mumbo-jumbo' (a synonym for gibberish in English), again are more African than Indian in origin, a *mumbo jumbo* being the tribal medicine man of central Africa who protected his people from evil. There is little doubt that Mrs. Bannerman drew her characters as she did not out of malice but because she was a conventional product of her era. A proper English gentlewoman of the '90s, one of the sustainers if not builders of the British Empire, she no doubt saw one dark-skinned non-Englishman as looking much like another. Indians and African blacks were readily and innocently confused in her mind.

Beyond the names and drawings in *Little Black Sambo,* surely nothing suggests a white-supremacist attitude. There is neither dialect nor anything in the least demeaning in the behavior of any character. Sambo's quick wit in moments of dire stress would be the envy of many a diplomat today. In a subsequent story by Mrs. Bannerman—*Kettlehead* (1904)—a small white heroine is far less sympathetically drawn. A foolish and disobedient child, she loses her head, in actuality, because she persists in disobeying her mother's warning to avoid playing with fire. Given a kettle by a frightened Indian servant who wishes to help her conceal the disastrous loss, Kettlehead easily fools her dull-witted English parents. They merely find it odd that their daughter never re-

moves her sunbonnet any more (it secures the kettle to her neck!).
Perhaps in later years Mrs. Bannerman herself even compre-
hended something of the unconscious condescension of specifying
Sambo as "black," for among her papers when she died was
found another story, unpublished during her lifetime, titled
Little White Squibba (as if to balance things on the eternal scales
of Justice), in which a small English heroine follows exactly
Sambo's course into the jungle but ends up, British-style, inviting
all the hungry tigers home to tea.

Far more interesting than the Sambo story itself (a good one
by any fair picture-book standards) are the reasons for its
phenomenal success in the United States. Surely it had something
to do with the fact that, for the first time, a story had caught
American parents and children off their guard, allowing them to
recognize freely the humanity of black people. Sambo's mother
sews him a beautiful coat and pair of trousers. His father buys
him "a lovely little Pair of Purple Shoes with Crimson Soles and
Crimson Linings" (I can still recall taking stock of the slippers
in our local shoe store as a child, hoping to find a pair exactly
like them). We could all approve of Sambo and his family without
feeling either guilty or anxious. Quick wit and intelligence were
no threat in a black boy from the primitive and faraway land of
tigers, as they might have been in someone black walking down an
American city street. Just as nature abhors a vacuum, so the
human soul rebels against evasion and dishonesty. By the time
Sambo arrived on these shores, the slaves had been free for some
forty years. Thousands of blacks had left the plantations of the
rural South to form an observable element in most cities' popula-
tions. Yet they might all have been invisible for the recognition
they received as fellow human beings in white America. Sambo

was taken to everyone's heart precisely because he allowed us to acknowledge what we knew inside but avoided confronting: that black people were human beings just like us. In loving Sambo unreservedly, in some way every white had the feeling that he was also accepting the black man as a fellow human being. The nursery bookshelf was integrated, and no prejudice could be said to exist in a home where *Little Black Sambo* and *Peter Rabbit* stood side by side on the same shelf.

Because *Little Black Sambo* unquestionably helped white American children and adults to see black people in a new way, possibly for the first time, the book was, on the whole, a positive force, just as, in their perverse ways, the "pickaninny dolls" which were sold in the United States in the 1930s and the golliwogs (the black-faced rag dolls which were a staple of the British toy market until very recently) also served to make white children recognize an otherwise unacknowledged fact—the existence in our own lives of black people—even if not in the most sensitive manner possible. Certain stereotypes are, on balance, broadening. Like the play and eventual radio series *Abie's Irish Rose,* or the popular soap opera of the '30s and '40s, *The Goldbergs* (graduated to television in the '50s), they often serve to make large numbers of perfectly ordinary persons, with the perfectly standard prejudices of their times, open eyes and ears just a little bit more than they might otherwise have done to realities they would rather not face.

As a teaching tool for white children, then, surely Sambo rated A-plus in his day. It would be both insensitive and hypocritical today, however, to accept the bland rationale offered in 1966 by an editor at Chatto & Windus (Mrs. Bannerman's English publishers) that "These stories belong to an entirely differ-

ent age. They're classically innocent. Certainly there is nothing
malicious about them.'' While the observation is wholly true, it
is also wholly irrelevant when balanced against a decade of
American films in which the black shoeshine boy was always called
Sambo, or, more recently, when placed beside the testimony—
exaggerated and misguided as some of it is—of the black Ne-
braska barber who said before a Presidential Riot Investigation
Commission in 1968:

> Here is what you are going to give my child. I am going to
> send him to school and teach him to respect authority. So
> here is a cracker teacher standing in front of my child mak-
> ing him listen to *Little Black Sambo*. See, that's the image
> the school gives him when he's young to teach him his
> ''place.'' A caricature, wearing outlandish clothing that
> even the animals in the forest don't want to wear. . . . All
> right. So he goes through the caricature like I did when I
> was a small child in grade school. . . . I sat through *Little
> Black Sambo*. And since I was the only black face in the
> room, I became Little Black Sambo. . . . Why don't you
> have Little Cracker Bohunk? Little Cracker Dago? Little
> Cracker Kike? You can't stand that. But you're going to
> take our little black children and expose them to this kind
> of ridicule, then not understand why we don't like it.

Poor Sambo does not deserve such criticism. He was black,
the hero of a beautifully satisfying picture book and, as such,
justly loved in his time. Realities and even fantasies shift, however, and those of the 1970s, for parents and children, have moved
a great distance from Sambo's lush green jungles to ones much
bleaker, more menacing and closer to home. As a period piece—a

163

relic of days when tigers roamed free outside of wild-animal refuges and mothers made pancakes from scratch—the work deserves to be preserved. As a fond memory of those of us over thirty, and white, it is unlikely to be forgotten. For the rest, one picture book is not worth a thousand angry protests. Let Sambo be consigned to literary history.

Sambo is not by himself in juvenile literary limbo. Our richest native store of black folk tales—those about Brer Rabbit as recorded in Joel Chandler Harris' Uncle Remus stories—has long been out of fashion both because of the difficult dialect in which it was written and, more, because of Uncle Remus himself, "an old darky" who tends to perpetuate the stereotype of "the slave's-in-his-cabin-and-all's-right-with-the-old-South." In 1967, however, the South Carolina poet Ennis Rees brought out the first of two superior Brer Rabbit picture books, *Brer Rabbit and His Tricks*. His selected tales, recast in a colloquial rhymed verse and effectively illustrated by Edward Gorey, live up to Mr. Rees's tribute that Brer Rabbit "remains our best example of how the small and weak can often outwit and thereby triumph over the large and powerful and hungry."

During 1967–68, several of Hugh Lofting's Dr. Dolittle books were studied by a member of the Council of Interracial Books for Children and found to be rife with white-supremacist attitudes that few Dolittle fans of a generation ago had ever consciously noted. The Spring-Summer 1968 issue of the group's publication, *Interracial Books for Children,* offered damning quotes from three Dolittle books, along with reproductions of typical illustrations of black native characters—all broad comic depictions. From *Dr. Dolittle's Post Office* there is cited the passage where King Koko of black Fantippo launches his new postal service with a letter to a former countryman "who runs a shoeshine parlor in Alabama." There is the unflattering implication that this job is neither more nor less exalted than being ruler of a tribe of ignorant savages. To those who grew up loving the Lofting works uncritically, indictments of this sort are rather like attacks on childhood. The tendency is loyally to defend such old favorites against minor blemishes thus magnified. We overlook the fact that these books posed no threat to (in fact, seldom even made contact with) our self-image as white children—except perhaps subtly to flatter it. But as Isabelle Sahl, the New York librarian who made the Dolittle survey, views it, "How many more generations of black children must be insulted by them and how many more white children allowed to be infected with their message of white superiority?"

For both children and adults, of course, literature has always served as a reflecting pool for contemporary social attitudes. Certainly blacks are not alone in their suffering at the hands of authors. Prior to the First World War (during that time when the *St. Nicholas* magazine was in its prime) American literature was strictly for the native-born. Irish immigrants were insensitively treated even earlier in the writings of such free-thinkers as Ralph Waldo Emerson or Henry David Thoreau. In general, new arrivals found their way into novels of quality only as maids or menials—with Irish brogue or Swedish accent—and served never as serious human portraits but merely for comic relief. And consider the case of the American Jew. From the writings of Edith Wharton, Theodore Dreiser, Sherwood Anderson and Willa Cather on up through F. Scott Fitzgerald, Ernest Hemingway and William Faulkner, he was treated first with open hostility, later with a gentlemanly contempt.

To comb the literature of the past for religious, ethnic or racial slurs, while always rewarding in terms of the ample evidence turned up, is also ultimately fruitless. One cannot seriously wish to edit the past or to banish otherwise rich and rewarding books for imperfections that are more a judgment on their creators and the societies that produced them than on the individuals or groups maligned. The central problem of prejudice—unconscious or blatant—when it appears in children's books is that we cannot expect from small children the objectivity of the Harlem teenager who, according to *The New York Times*'s Gertrude Samuels, was questioned about the reference to Huckleberry Finn's friend Jim as "Miss Watson's big nigger named Jim," and was able to say:

"Well, I feel this way. I feel that a hundred years ago when Mark Twain wrote this book, Negroes were slaves and there was no way to write about slaves except the way he said it, 'Nigger.' In this era, I would see it differently."

It is on "this era," happily, that most individuals and organizations concerned with the black image projected in books for young children are concentrating their major effort. James Baldwin has spoken movingly of American black children as having "a feeling of no past, no present and no future." Unlike immigrant groups, American blacks never came to these shores by choice. Cruelly cut off from family and tribal cultures once sold into slavery, they had little to fall back on when the outside world proved openly hostile or, at best, callously indifferent. As slaves, American blacks were merely property; after slavery, those newly declared citizens were ill-equipped to melt gradually into the general population (as other minority groups before and after them did) by reason of their prior deprivations and their high physical visibility. The nation and its dominant white population dealt with this thorny problem for close to a hundred years, in literature as elsewhere, by pretending that it did not exist. Before the 1950s, there was only the merest handful of books for children dealing with the subject of race, even obliquely. One of the most touching of these was a modest alphabet book by the black painter and illustrator Charles C. Dawson, who wrote, illustrated and probably himself published the *ABC's of Great Negroes* in Chicago in 1933. Dawson lists a number of obvious choices—George Washington Carver, Frederick Douglass and Booker T. Washington—as well as a number of locally prominent black men he knew in Chicago. Where the letters prove too difficult, he falls back upon the ready store of Egyptian pharaohs and Ethiopian potentates. Uneasy about doing this, however, he closes the book with a long explanatory footnote full of a quiet and pathetic irony:

> The ancient Ethiopians and Egyptians are unmistakably of the racial stock known today as Negroes. . . . Much confusion has been developed in modern times by most writers in the absurd attempt to confine the Negro race to one type, despite the fact like all of the great racial groups, the Negro race is made up of a large variety of types. . . . Truly, if the rule used by these writers for determining a Negro should be applied to the American Negro, he could very largely be claimed as part or variation of the great caucasian family instead of being what he is, in fact, a Negroid.

It was only during the 1950s that blacks truly began to speak as free men with certain inalienable rights. And if in children's literature as elsewhere today, their reactions seem oversensitive, misguided and, on occasion, even paranoid, they must be taken on faith as arising from experiences that the rest of us are only dimly beginning to comprehend. Precisely because no positive self-image can be taken for granted in the black child who opens a book (the direct opposite is more likely to be the case), it is not unreasonable to find an exquisite concern that whatever references to black men appear should enhance rather than diminish a child's sense of selfhood.

At the beginning of the 1960s, Whitney Young, Jr., justly pointed out that, on the most basic level, black faces were not represented in children's books in their proper proportion to the general population of the United States. As an example, he cited a new picture book about the city of Chicago in which a crowd scene at the Chicago zoo revealed not a single black face. Picking up Mr. Young's cue, Nancy Larrick reported in a *Saturday Review* piece in 1965 ("The All-White World of Children's Books") that in the three-year period 1962–65, out of 5,206 juvenile books published, only 349, or 6.7 percent, had any black characters in them. The four publishers with the largest juvenile lists had blacks in only 4.2 percent of their books. The situation steadily improved, of course, in this respect during the next five years. Slowly, a plurality of picture books began to display a casual sprinkling of black faces—almost too casual, as if a knowing cook were merely adding pinches of salt or pepper to every recipe as a reflex reaction. It was too painless a solution for one hundred years of separation and exclusion. Integration was not simply a matter of recognizing an existing problem and subjecting it to a saturation bombardment of smiling good will. Observant white viewers dutifully noticed these new black children in the classrooms, playgrounds and neighborhoods pictured in books; but since the discreetly shaded newcomers were often indistinguishable in dress, activity, look and place of residence from the book's white characters, black children occasionally missed the point. A teacher with one of these mid-'60s picture books in hand asked the children in her predominantly black classroom if they noticed anything different about the book before them. There was no immediate response, but finally one child cautiously volunteered: "Well, a lot of the children are sunburned."

As Julius Lester, the black author of *To Be a Slave, Search for the New Land* and *Black Folk Tales,* noted of such books, "There were a few with black faces on one or two pages, but those black faces were nothing more than white faces painted brown. If anything looks worse than an idealized drawing of a white child, it is an idealized drawing of a black one. There was absolutely nothing black about the children in the books. They looked like chocolate white kids, talked like white kids and thought like white kids. But we shrugged and said, well, something is better than nothing."

Something is assuredly better than nothing. The books express and even give pictorial credence to an ideal: the fully integrated society. To the extent, however, that the comforting picture they present deflects the attention of white children and adults from less pleasing racial realities, they are harmful. Also, when the picture presented—of effortless integration, the instant mixing of the races—is so far from the truth as to give black children no sense of their own lives and real hopes, then their purpose is entirely defeated. As late as May 1969, Augusta Baker, Coordinator of the Office of Children's Services of the New York Public Library, herself black, wrote of the swelling tide of such books: "I would hope that we would not take a manuscript and go through every third page and paint one child and every fourth family black to integrate the book."

Of what, then, does a proper "blackness"—neither Samboism nor color-me-brown—consist? Surely, thus far, the desire and effort to provide needed books on the subject of race have led less to a wider contentment than to still further controversy and contention. In 1968 the well-known black artist Jacob Lawrence wrote and illustrated *Harriet and the Promised Land* (Simon and Schuster), a simple, stark picture book about Harriet Tubman, who was born a slave in Maryland in 1822 and led more then three hundred of her fellow slaves north to freedom. Julius Lester, who read the book to his nursery-school-age daughter, had only praise for the work. It "confronted her," he felt, "with an aspect of what it means to be black. The distorted convoluted paintings did not confuse or dismay her." Yet a young black woman, active in a number of black causes, was outraged by Lawrence's epic and stylized conception of illustration. "What is that man drawing? Blacks just don't look like that! His slaves are something out of a white man's minstrel show, not human beings. He's been brainwashed by white America and lost touch with himself, that's a fact."

Lester, perhaps more sensitive to Lawrence's intent and achievement in *Harriet,* further noted: "Well, man . . . you have to explain it. My child wanted to know about all kinds of things . . . what chariots were . . . why Harriet's hand was so big. So I asked her, 'Did you ever walk so long that your feet felt they were as big as your body? That's how Harriet felt when she was scrubbing floors.' " Here Lester has hit on something fundamental to all books for small children. On the one hand, there is the book and its author's experience. Then, there is also the adult reader and his experience. The superior children's book will often unlock something in the adult reader's experience and, one hopes, make it available to the child listener. The hearer is then doubly blessed.

Sometimes, too, whites have proved more sensitive than blacks to possible racial slights. Ezra Jack Keats, who has since 1963 written a number of graphically handsome and unpretentious picture books with a small black hero, Peter (beginning with *The Snowy Day*), was criticized for this first book by Nancy Larrick because Peter's mother was, to her eyes, stereotyped, "a huge figure in a gaudy yellow-plaid dress, albeit without a red bandana."

An incensed Keats replied: "The dress is gaily colored as is everything else in the book. What is wrong with a mother being 'huge'? What if she were white? I wish Miss Larrick would not project upon me the stereotypes in her own mind—or in others. If she sees a figure of a large Negro mother and associates it with a red bandana, that is her problem, not mine."

It is, of course, everybody's problem to some extent. Great numbers of blacks and whites—the vast majority of both races—have a minimal understanding of one another. I can remember, on one of my many jobs in· New York City, being employed by a small museum that still retained some of the elegant furnishings of the town house it had once been. The office which I shared with a black secretary had a magnificent room-size Persian rug on the floor and we more than once remarked on its exceptional beauty. One morning, as it was being rolled up for a semi-annual floor waxing, my black colleague said in all seriousness: "That sure is *some* rug. I bet it would cost more than $75 to get one anywhere

near like it.'' I was appalled by the disparity between her knowledge and mine about even one insignificant fact of life in the
world we shared. Books on race, particularly for children, must be
willing to acknowledge and confront all manner of particular differences, as well as broad similarities, if the chasm between white
and black is truly to narrow.

In the spring of 1970, there were 134 books submitted for consideration in the picture-book division of the thirty-fourth Annual
Spring Children's Book Festival sponsored by *Book World.* Of
134 books submitted, 35, or more than 25 percent (including the
first-prize winner), contained black characters, at least in the
background. In 14 of the books, a black character was more than
peripheral, and in 8 cases, blacks were the heroes. In 7 books, a
black character was a close friend or next-door neighbor to a white
child. In 2 books, black policemen were depicted; in one a black
veterinarian; in another a black school principal; and in still
others, a black mailman, a draftsman and a philosopher-gardener.
In what was a wholly logical and inspired move on the part of the
artist Janusz Grabianski, Androcles was depicted as a black
African in a 1970 edition of *Androcles and the Lion* (Watts).
Another book, with an all-black cast and written and illustrated by
a black husband and wife, Muriel and Tom Feelings—*Zamani
Goes to Market* (Seabury)—depicts a small black boy taking a
first step toward manhood in the stable and structured society of
a Nigerian village. Zamani's father and brothers are all-important
models for him, and the courtly manners of each member of the
family toward every other are most pleasing to observe. Yet another book, *Freddie Found a Frog* (Van Nostrand), tells of a
small black boy in a contemporary urban setting discovering and

protecting a small frog. No child, black or white, is likely to recognize Freddie's city backyard, complete with a mother out of *Vogue* (Mrs. Larrick take note!) and a lily pond out of the author's purest fancy.

Two books containing fairy—not folk—tales with black heroes seemed a promising development, particularly when one recalls the unhappy black Prince Bumpo in *The Story of Dr. Dolittle*. (A constant reader of fairy tales, Bumpo ardently daydreams, "If only I were a white prince.") What better way to enhance any child's self-image than through identification with the traditional princes and princesses of fairyland? Joan Balfour Payne's *The Raven and Other Fairy Tales* (Hastings House) was perhaps the simplest and most winning collection in this genre for youngest readers. *Princess of the Full Moon* by Frederic Guirma (Macmillan) is a more elaborate single fairy tale of authentic African— Upper Volta—derivation for slightly older readers.

Do more recent books, then, achieve the necessary balance of blackness, or are they, in their way, still at some remove from the central core of American black-white realities? Theodore Dolmatch, president of the Pitman Publishing Corporation, has branded these efforts as obvious "separate but equal books," designed not to widen the area of black-white human contacts but rather to entrench our distance from one another. Can literature in fact play any meaningful role in redressing long-standing social injustice? Isaac Bashevis Singer has commented that "When a writer tries to teach a lesson, he achieves nothing as an artist and nothing as a propagandist," but this is not wholly true. Many books for blacks today are assuredly propaganda of sorts; yet occasionally they also achieve something. *Some of the Days of*

EVALINE NESS *Some of the Days of Everett Anderson*

Everett Anderson, by the black poet Lucille Clifton (Holt, Rine-hart & Winston), is a case in point. A modest collection of poems about an ordinary boy, it is reminiscent of A. A. Milne's *When We Were Very Young* or *Now We Are Six.* Everett Anderson, like other small boys, turns chairs into motorcycles, listens to night noises with imagination running free, and dips his finger into his mother's beer—all convincingly illustrated by Evaline Ness—but he is also unmistakably black, as in his self-conscious poem:

> Afraid of the dark
> is afraid of Mom
> and Daddy
> and Papa
> and Cousin Tom.
>
> "I'd be as silly
> as I could be,
> afraid of the dark
> is afraid of Me!"
>
> says ebony
> Everett
> Anderson.

A nice conceit, it is propaganda, and perhaps a little bit more, that needs saying. In many a black-market-oriented book today, one sees the message writ large: black boys are as sensitive as white; black children love and need their fathers; black children are intelligent and responsible. Of course they are, and if it is said often and well enough, one day blacks and whites alike will believe it, too.

In the fall of 1969, a promising young black author-artist from the Bedford-Stuyvesant area of Brooklyn, John Steptoe, wrote and illustrated a new and rather special slice-of-life story directed at black children. *Stevie* (Harper & Row) was, as he explained, the sort of book black children ''could read without translating the language, something real which would relate to what a black child would know.'' But not only did Steptoe's language seem real to many black children reading his story, it also struck a clear note of recognition—and truth—for many white children in cities who knew black children in their classes who spoke in precisely the cadences Steptoe captured. ''He was smaller than me.'' . . . ''Is that them?'' . . . ''My momma don't call me Robertie.'' . . . ''But why I gotta take him everywhere I go?'' . . . Here, at last, was a recognizable human being drawn from life. Steptoe's *Stevie* was not intended for white children, but the tale it tells— of sibling rivalry and the realization by an older boy that a nuisance of a small brother adds considerable spice to life—has universal appeal. After Stevie leaves, the hero of the tale recalls ''the time we played boogie man and we hid under the covers with Daddy's flashlight.'' And the closing line, ''Aw, no! I let my cornflakes get soggy thinkin' about him,'' brings not black or white but universal laughter.

It must cause real pain in many an editor and literate parent (a pain experienced and expressed by writers and readers during earlier periods of social change in the United States) that even language is required to yield and accommodate itself to new usages and mis-usages by new groups of Americans. No one can deny that some of the precision and elegance of English, as literate white and black Americans have spoken it, may be lost temporarily and possibly permanently as language gives voice to new life styles and aspirations. No real social gains have ever been made by the dispossessed without genuine changes affecting those who possess—their schools, their neighborhoods, and their language and literature as well. What is lost is always regained somehow in new and unexpected ways.

No doubt, one day in the future, such books as Steptoe's *Stevie* and his more recent *Uptown,* written in a current street style that is ever changing, will seem as dated, and even condescending, as Leo Rosten's *The Education of H*Y*M*A*N K*A*P*L*A*N* with its heavily Yiddish-accented English. Yet, such books serve, in their time, as remarkably useful instruments to broaden understanding and sympathy.

"He who wishes to create an authentic work of art must realize that the truths of a nation are in the first place its realities," Frantz Fanon once wrote. "He must go on until he has found the seething pot out of which the learning of the future will emerge." Or, in words more suited to books for the young, Ezra Jack Keats has said, "All people want is the opportunity to be people. Let us open the book covers, these long-shut doors, to new and wonderful, true and inspiring books for all children; about all children—the tall and short, fat and thin, dark and light, beautiful and homely. Welcome!"

ANITA LOBEL *The Little Wooden Farmer*

12: Once Upon the Timeless: The Enduring Power of a Child's First Books

What is Patriotism but the love of the good things we ate in our childhood?

LIN YUTANG

ONG, LONG AGO, mothers and fathers were little girls and boys, just as you are now. . . .'' It falls within the realm of the magical to children that this fact can possibly be true. To be a young child is to be locked in an ever advancing present, to find it almost impossible to imagine what the world could have been like—or, indeed, that it could really have existed at all—without oneself as its observer. Thus, when parents tell children of events from the parents' own childhoods, the recollections already have, to the small listeners, the character of romance and myth. Beyond this, all grownups invariably polish or embellish their own pasts. In the telling of events from childhood, there creep in touches of nostalgia for what is gone—for youth if nothing else—and a selectivity born of maturity, or perhaps of a kind of grown-up didacticism which must extract some pattern and lesson from the muddle of bygone events.

To children, who begin by knowing only their own sensations and the world as an extension of themselves, all stories—be they parental recollections of past facts, fairy tales, animal fables or alphabet books—require a determined effort toward objectivity, a recognition that the world exists independent of the self. First books, then, always occupy a special, an almost magical plane to small children. Beyond the next few hours, the future has no real meaning and the past is entirely personal, inextricably entwined in the developing self. This perhaps explains in part why so many of the most memorable children's books take place outside of any specifically identifiable time or place and have about them an air of the everlasting now. From *Little Red Riding Hood* to Charlotte Zolotow's *Mr. Rabbit and the Lovely Present,* the tales happen in a generalized space and time. Peter Rabbit's family lives now and forever "in a sand-bank, underneath the root of a very big fir tree," just as Goldie Rosenzweig in M. B. Goffstein's *Goldie the Dollmaker* will continue "with her father's work of carving small wooden dolls, and her mother's work of painting bright clothes and friendly faces on them" so long as children continue to read her story. They have about them, as childhood does, an aura of the immortal.

This quality of timelessness is one of the enduring seductions of the literature of early childhood, and it can provide the fortunate child with strong spiritual fortification against future buffeting in life's school of hard knocks. Paul Hazard, that great French romanticist of childhood in our century, saw children's books as providing "insurance against the time, all too soon, when there will be nothing but realities." Lucky, then, the small child who has for his own lullaby Yulya's *Bears are Sleeping* or who is mesmerized into slumber viewing Jean Charlot's cosily blurry-eyed illustrations in Margaret Wise Brown's *A Child's Good Night Book.* Happy, too, is he who has gained insight into the irreconcilable world views of parent and child from Mary Chalmers' wise and funny *Throw a Kiss, Harry,* or acquired a glimmer of the charm of just words from Louis Slobodkin's *Mr. Mushroom.*

Often, particularly with small children, an adult will choose a book for its likely subject matter: steam shovels, fire engines, teddy bears, dragons or fairy princesses—whatever may be the child's interest of the day or week. The quality of the writing scarcely enters into consideration. And frequently, as the grownup labors through a turgid text, he hopes against hope that the child will not approve the choice, since the thought of rereading the book is almost more than the adult can bear. Yet, certain books have an almost guaranteed appeal for smallest children, with or without literary quality. *The Little Engine That Could* (in the Platt and Munk telling by Watty Piper, with illustrations by George and Doris Hauman) is such a work. Its text, with a pleasing, repetitive cadence and the high suspense of witnessing the breakdown and agony of a little train whose cars are "filled full of good things for boys and girls," holds most two-to-four-year-olds rapt throughout. Will all "the good little boys and girls on the other side of the mountain" ever receive their just reward? It's touch-and-go until a little blue engine finally volunteers for the arduous climb over the mountain, gamely puffing, "I think I can—I think I can—I think I can." Only a child with a chronic case of the stomach ache is able to resist sharing the final triumph as the engine rolls down to the valley beyond, chugging, "I thought I could. I thought I could. I thought I could."

Small children find catharsis in such stories which gently probe and ultimately confirm the benign nature of the universe. Other books, like Lois Lenski's *The Little Train* and Alice Dalgliesh's *The Little Wooden Farmer* (the 1968 edition is hand-

181

LOIS LENSKI *The Little Train*

somely illustrated by Anita Lobel), skillfully blend simple facts and toy-town illustrations, never bothering to raise a ripple of doubt concerning the predictable workings of a bustling, perfectly ordered world. Though adults are likely to find them pedestrian and dull, particularly to read again and again, these tales fulfill the small child's need to acquire increasing bits of knowledge, as well as his craving for the world about him to be both purposeful and explicable. Such books are often requested for bedtime reading and remembered for years, occasionally forming the basis for a child's first real efforts at matching specific words with memorized text—the most magical beginning of reading for the lucky few.

In books for three-to-six-year-olds, it is difficult, sometimes impossible, to separate the words from the art, or the combination from the over-all conception, size and format of the work. All are components of its enduring voice. Often the illustration isolated from the book as a whole is disappointingly slight. Take Mary Chalmers' simple line drawings for her charming trilogy about an independent kitten named Harry (*Throw a Kiss, Harry; Take a Nap, Harry;* and *Be Good, Harry*). By themselves they are unimpressive, inconsequential. Yet, when taken together with the books' small format, the brief texts and the author's sound and subtle observations of the eternal tug-of-war between the desires and purposes of parents and their children, the sum makes three wholly beguiling and deeply truthful tales. "Boy, that sure is one stubborn cat!" my six-year-old son observed admiringly, delighting in Harry's passive but firm resistance to his mother's order to "Throw a kiss or I'll tell your father to give you a spanking when you get home."

The appeal of a book like M. B. Goffstein's *Sleepy People*

183

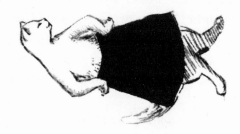

MARY CHALMERS *Throw a Kiss, Harry*

M . B . G O F F S T E I N *Sleepy People*

can only be explained in terms of the artist-author's unique conception. The notion of a minuscule, droopy-lidded race, some of whose members may be "living in one of your old bedroom slippers," is inspired, helping to make her small work a rival to the sandman in summoning slumber. The success of Uri Shulevitz's urban fantasy *One Monday Morning* also turns on that author-illustrator's droll conception: the incongruity of a royal entourage—king, queen, prince, knight and palace retinue in full panoply—proceeding regally down a rundown city block, then huddling in a tenement hallway, looking for the doorbell of the little boy they inexplicably come to visit each day of the week.

The voice of a small child's book may linger because of qualities as frail as the satisfying alliteration to be found in Louis Slobodkin's delicately wrought saga, *Mr. Mushroom*. A quartet of friends—Mr. Mole, Mr. Mouse, Mr. Moth and Miss Mite—attend Mr. Mushroom's wedding, "eat MUSH and MARSHMALLOWS," "drink MILK! Of course," and dance the "MINUET" by the light of the moon until morning.

Or the appeal may be almost wholly visual. There are Bruno

Munari's large-format picture books which speak directly to the imagination through their graphic invention and wit. Consisting of six to eight heavy board pages, each of Munari's books provides surprising new vistas of visual possibility to children. There is *The Birthday Present,* which is like opening present after surprising present any time you feel like it, not only on your birthday. There is *The Elephant's Wish,* in which the viewer can peep into the minds of several beasts and birds and be privy to their innermost thoughts. There are also *Tic, Tac,* and *Toc,* a delightful trio of terse bird biographies within one large book, and *Jimmy Has Lost His Cap,* which is like playing a suspenseful game of solo hide-and-go-seek. The world itself seems more magical on closing one of his mind-expanding inventions.

An unassuming voice like author-illustrator Berthe Amoss' in *Tom in the Middle,* on the other hand, may be remembered not because of its imaginative depth or high originality but because it so truly captures the triumphs and defeats of being a middle child, the constantly shifting alliances within a family of three children. Admittedly, it is not the stuff of Homer's *Odyssey,* but the indelible memories of childhood are often closer to the pains Mrs. Amoss chronicles: being called "Stupid!" at a vulnerable moment; or the ignominy of having been found out playing with an older brother or sister's cherished Monopoly set because one "got all the $100 bills mixed up with the $500s."

Part of many a book's lingering "voice" for youngest children is its size. Both the smallest and largest picture books often start off with a built-in appeal. In the case of the first, the child is able easily to manage the book by himself and feels well disposed toward its contents. It belongs to him alone as he turns the pages. Small illustrations not only require close attention but give

URI SHULEVITZ *One Monday Morning*

ESTEBAN FRANCES *The Thread Soldier*

the child a simultaneous sense of kinship with, and command over, whatever is pictured. My younger son delighted in poring over the pages of a small book called *The Thread Soldier* by Anne Heathers with illustrations by Esteban Frances. He loved the hero who magically materialized from an unwinding spool of thread and also thoroughly enjoyed the suspense and horror of seeing him nearly unraveled by an offstage villainess. *Susanna's Auction* by Louis-Maurice Boutet de Monvel is another small work where the child's sympathy for an unregenerate bad girl is in part assured by the perfect fit of book size and format to the crime its pages reveal. By the same token, an outsize volume, which cries out for the lap and page-turning services of a grownup to unlock the treasures within, also induces an attentive and receptive state of mind in small listeners. If the tiny picture book can be compared to a whisper, the outsize one is a shout. It commands attention. Opening one of Selina Chonz's Alpine sagas with their beckoning illustrations by Alois Carigiet—*A Bell for Ursli* or *The Snowstorm*—is like stepping into Switzerland for the tale's duration. Large-format books prove particularly effective where the small child's attention is being drawn to a variety of factual details. The colorful and popular picture geographies of various cities of the world by Miroslav Sasek (*This Is London, This Is Paris,* etc.) neither tire nor bore most small children precisely because of the artful use of the white space surrounding each closely observed architectural detail or idiosyncrasy of custom or dress. The same is true of Richard Scarry's volumes for small children, those pictorial encyclopedias of costume, tools, foods, human habitations, occupations and means of locomotion.

Surely even Beatrix Potter's memorable voice derives in part from the scale of her artwork and size of her books. In *The Tale of Two Bad Mice,* Hunca Munca and her husband, Tom Thumb, take up residence in a doll's house. The story's chief delight lies not so much in its words as in the exquisite touches Miss Potter achieves within her miniature world. The reader automatically shrinks to mouse scale to discover with the dollhouse inhabitants that the food in the larder "underneath the shiny paint . . . was made of nothing but plaster." And Miss Potter has us look out, with the wondering eyes of Tom Thumb, at the dollhouse roof and find there a common housefly transformed into a creature of fantasy simply because it has been accurately drawn in ordinary lifesize scale.

Miss Potter's voice owes much as well, of course, to her prose style. Consider the economy and understatement of Mrs. Rabbit's instructions to her four children in *The Tale of Peter Rabbit:* " 'Now, my dears,' said old Mrs. Rabbit one morning, 'you may go into the fields or down the lane, but don't go into Mr. McGregor's garden: your Father had an accident there; he was put in a pie by Mrs. McGregor.' "

Not the least of Miss Potter's charms was her gift of taking her tales and her small readers seriously, speaking to the latter as equals. Thus, at the close of *The Tale of Johnny Town-Mouse,* the author confides to the reader without a hint of condescension: "One place suits one person, another place suits another person. For my part I prefer to live in the country, like Timmie Willie." And the child listener, for his part, is entirely free to decide the matter for himself.

Boutet de Monvel addressed his readers in much the same no-nonsense, adult fashion. At the start of his memorable picture book *Joan of Arc,* he says forthrightly: "Her history will teach you that in order to conquer, you must believe that you will conquer.'' It is a sober statement, in keeping with the stately purity of this French author-illustrator's conception of his heroine and her exploits. His speaking voice is always in perfect harmony with the muted colors, the elegance of line and beauty of execution in each epic illustration for this monument of picture-book art. The work's voice has the unique dignity of the heroine it depicts.

Those voices children hear earliest and remember longest are, as often as not, lighthearted. In *I'll Fix Anthony,* author Judith Viorst offers a fantasy about sibling rivalry in which a younger brother confides to the reader: ''Mother says deep down in his heart Anthony loves me. Anthony says deep down in his heart he thinks I stink.'' My two sons found the lines hilarious because they daily live with its truth. Liesel Moak Skorpen in *That Mean Man* creates for us a hero so unlovable that ''When he had something nice like jelly beans, he didn't share. When he had something nasty like chicken pox, he did.'' And Edward Ardizzone, in *The Wrong Side of the Bed,* tells, without words, of a little boy who can do no right on one black day of his life. After a scolding by his father, he sulkily leaves the house, picturing his father's face mounted on the body of a fat pig. We are at once shocked and delighted by this truthful glimpse into our secret selves.

The best of the voices that speak to us from children's books surprise us and expand our sense of life's possibilities as well as our understanding of ourselves. Surely Tomi Ungerer must rank high here. ''Never be discouraged,'' he tells us in *The Mellops Go Flying,* his first story, in 1957, ''the Mellops are not.'' And every subsequent Ungerer work bears out this irrepressible philosophy of life. Though his tales are brimful of disaster—fires, accidents, mechanical breakdowns, threats by felons and ogres—

EDWARD ARDIZZONE *The Wrong Side of the Bed*

his heroes always win out in the end. His flying kangaroo, Adelaide, nearly dies of heroism; Zeralda falls into the clutches of a
terrible, child-eating ogre; and in a recent work, *The Hat,* a
dashing young cadet, while "entertaining a young mother with
fresh gossip," flicks the ashes of his fat cigar into an occupied
baby carriage and almost incinerates its innocent occupant. But
despite Ungerer's clear-eyed documentation of the folly and wickedness rampant in the world, tragedy is always narrowly averted.
The excitement he provides is out of the daily range of experience
of most well-cared-for children and responsible adults, but it always seems to be within the realm of life's larger possibilities,
the very ones that cause us all so much hidden anxiety. We close
every Ungerer book with a sense of optimism and release: whatever life may have in store, good or bad, it can be overcome if we
follow the example of the Mellops, Adelaide, Zeralda or Benito
Badoglio, the portly hero of *The Hat.*

As the child grows beyond the age of four, words increasingly become the focus of his interest in books. The irony contained in Richard Hughes's topsy-turvy world of *Gertrude's
Child,* a tale in which dolls and animals possess children, will not
escape him. Note the arrival of two guests at a hastily arranged
birthday party:

> Next came a puppydog, dragging a small boy behind him on
> a rope. The puppydog marched straight in without even say-
> ing "Howdy" to Gertrude and jumped up into a chair at the
> table where the food was spread out. The little boy tried to
> climb up beside him, but "Lie down!" barked the puppydog
> to the little boy. "Or you'll be tied up outside and not have
> any cookies at all!"

193

TOMI UNGERER *The Hat*

Voices like Isaac Bashevis Singer's in *Mazel and Schlimazel* can be appreciated in all their subtlety, as when the Princess Nesika discusses with her father why she has rejected her latest suitor:

Nesika had simply announced that she would not have him because his boots were foolish.

"How can boots be foolish?" her father asked.

"If the feet are foolish, the boots are foolish," Nesika replied.

"How can feet be foolish?" her father insisted.

"If the head is foolish, the feet are foolish," Nesika retorted.

At six and seven, the child finds in the tales of Hans Christian Andersen and the Brothers Grimm more than he had grasped from simplified picture-book versions. And works like Oscar Wilde's *The Happy Prince* may encourage him to stretch his understanding to its outermost limits, straining to comprehend the full meaning behind such words as:

"When I was alive and had a human heart," answered the statue, "I did not know what tears were, for I lived in the Palace of Sans-Souci, where sorrow is not allowed to enter. In the daytime I played with my companions in the garden, and in the evening I led the dance in the Great Hall. Round the garden ran a very lofty wall, but I never cared to ask what lay beyond it, everything about me was so beautiful. My courtiers called me the Happy Prince, and happy indeed I was, if pleasure be happiness. So I lived, and so I died. And now that I am dead they have set me up here so high that I can see all the ugliness and all the misery of my city, and though my heart is made of lead yet I cannot choose but weep."

It is at this point that the child reaches the threshold of literature as the adult world judges it.

Henry James once wrote of his friend Robert Louis Stevenson: "He doesn't speak as a parent, or an uncle, or an educator—he speaks as a contemporary completely absorbed in his own game." And it is this quality of being a contemporary "completely absorbed in his own game" which generally characterizes the truly resonant voices of childhood reading. The memorable writers and illustrators hold nothing back. They give us not what they think we ought to have but what has meaning to themselves. They follow the rule that Stevenson did in his *Treasure Island:* "It's awful fun, boys' stories. You just indulge the pleasure of your heart."

Suppose, however, we are the sort of parents who frown upon this view of books as "awful fun" written by authors indulging the pleasure of their hearts. Like Mr. Gradgrind, the schoolmaster of Dickens' *Hard Times,* we may proclaim:

"Now what I want is Facts. Teach these boys and girls nothing but Facts. Facts alone are wanted in life. Plant nothing else, and root out everything else. You can only form the minds of reasoning animals upon Facts. Nothing else will ever be of any service to them. . . ."

But as soon as we look closely at these "reasoning animals," our small children, we find that the "facts" of their everyday lives do not in any way corroborate a reasonable view of life. Consider the small child who has just learned to walk—in itself a wholly magical accomplishment from his point of view. Concentrating on his forward motion, he may see a barrier—a door— before him. But, because his attention is concentrated on remaining upright and, in any case, because his eye is below doorknob level, he does not see the adult hand that reaches over his head to open the door. All he knows is that the barrier, magically, disappears on his arrival. What a sense of mystery, perhaps even power, it must give him. By the same token, such magic often works entirely in reverse. While he is contentedly playing on the floor, absorbed in some fascinating child work of his own, adult arms will, from nowhere, reach down and scoop him up, perhaps to plunk him into a bathtub—the furthest thought from his busy mind. As powerful as he felt in the first instance, he must now experience a sense of frustration and impotence. No doubt this is part of the perennial fascination stories about kings and wicked witches who wield absolute and often arbitrary power have for small children. The familiar world of childhood is magical to children, and the route to adult realities lies in recognizing and utilizing that magic.

It is difficult, if not impossible, to know which of the myriad of children's books will penetrate a given child's own magic circle of existence and strike the clarion note of pure truth. "No one can possibly tell what tiny detail of a drawing or what seemingly trivial phrase in a story will be the spark that sets off a great flash in the mind of some child," Robert Lawson said in his 1941 acceptance speech for the Caldecott Medal, "a flash that will leave a glow there until the day he dies." Children are notoriously quirky in their observations, and unpredictable about the things that touch them deeply. When I was very young, my parents attended a formal New Year's Eve party at a Boston nightclub called The Russian Bear. For some reason, that name struck me as the most romantic one on earth—partly, I think, because it was the first time I was aware of my parents being so handsomely dressed. To this day, I have an ashtray they brought home from that party and remain partial to children's stories about bears.

Then, too, I can remember the time my younger brother flatly refused to go to nursery school for a whole week because he had been frightened by the teacher's brother, who had paid the class a casual visit. A formidably tall twenty-year-old, he had enormous feet and a deep, reverberating voice. At three, my brother could not see much higher than the visitor's knees, and somehow he determined that the voice emanated from the outsize shoes, a revelation that filled him with terror for days to come.

It was E. B. White who defined a child's mind as a "repository full of gems of questionable merit, paste and real, held in storage," and Sir Arthur Quiller-Couch who wrote in the preface of a collection of Arthur Rackham's illustrations that: "The child's Heaven, like the child's earth, is a mixture of the mysterious and the definite, the practical and the absurd. . . . He wants to know how creation was managed . . . to see the wheels go round . . . who made the trees, life, guardsmen, the sea, porridge, jam, uncles and aunts. . . ."

Surely all small children labor to make some sense of the world they inhabit and are constantly adjusting their views as they come into possession of new facts, from life or books. Robert Lawson observed, "The children of three or four whom I know are rational beings, anything less infantile I can't imagine. . . . There are no non-sequiturs [in their thoughts]—there are always links." But think of the welter of facts, misinformation, misconception and fears with which small children must work. When I was six or seven, an entire summer at the shore was blighted when an older boy told me, after I had accidentally stepped on a white jellyfish, that I was sure to die before reaching the age of thirteen. It was simply the fate of anyone dumb enough to step on white jellyfish. I believed him wholly. I remember, too, a terrible time at approximately the same age when I was taken to the circus by my mother. Our seats were high up in the stands, and somehow, in straining to see the action in the rings far below, my eyes came to focus on my own nose in a way they never had before. For days afterward I simply could not take my eyes off it: the world became an extension of my own nose. And, making sense of the facts at my command, I decided this was a curse unique to me. My eyes being the only ones in the world subject to so bizarre a malfunction, it was certain I had some rare and awful malady. Nose-watching was a warning sign of incipient blindness. Frightened as I was, however, I would never have dreamed of revealing my fears to my unsuspecting parents.

While parents doubtless provide great comfort to their children at numberless times in their lives, it is equally true that children are often least able to make their deepest feelings and worries known to them. As André Maurois observed of the Disraeli children's attitude toward their mother in his biography of Benjamin: "They adored her and told her not a word of what was nearest to their hearts." Often a book—even a most unlikely one —is uncannily able to approach those secret regions of affect when nothing else can. Rudyard Kipling, in reminiscing about his own miserable boyhood in London, referred to the power of certain books to rouse memories in children, even to resolve long dormant pains and fears they were unaware of harboring. Literature provides the cool, detached voice that parents seldom can.

We may, all of us, intend to be our children's friends and confidants, but it is simply not possible. The voice that calls a child to dinner, demands that hands be washed and dirty socks thrown into the washing machine, cannot always adjust itself to tones of sympathy and understanding when they are most needed. For one thing, parents become prisoners of their role, an observable fact that severely limits their influence in many areas of their children's lives. When my own children were very young, we lived for some summers in the country house of an eminent historian. At the age of eighty, he finally sold this house and, with it, many of its rustic furnishings and decorations. Among these was an oil painting one of his daughters had done as a teenager, perhaps thirty years earlier. The work revealed undeniable flaws of composition and technique, and her father, noting these, appended a note to the frame which said: "This was done by my daughter M—— and is not wholly satisfactory. I wish there were time to have her do it over." The note was both absurd and poignantly truthful. Parents, at eighty, are unable to divest themselves of the eternal parental stance, one full of anxiety for their children's performance in life.

Yet, even in moments of genuine rapport and confidence, we do not always feel adequate to our children's needs. It was E. B. White who noted:

Much of our adult morality, in books and out of them, has a stuffiness unworthy of childhood. Our grown-up conclusions often rest on perilously soft bottom. Try to tell a child even the simplest truth about planetary, cosmical or spiritual things, and you hear strange echoes in your head. "Can this be me?" a voice keeps asking, "Can this be me?" Dozens of times in the course of trying to act like a parent I have caught myself telling my boy things I didn't thoroughly comprehend myself, urging him toward conventional attitudes of mind and spirit I only half believed in and would myself gladly chuck overboard.

The memorable books of childhood are those that managed somehow to cut through cant and convention to say simply that thing our spirits thirsted to hear at a given moment. The reason why one child's favorite may be no one else's is that the meeting of a book and a child's individual need is a fragile and fortuitous happening. We all may have sat docilely—even attentively—through readings of the books our parents wanted us to hear, but each of us was most deeply touched by the few that said what we were waiting to hear at a particular instant in our development. Kate Greenaway wisely observed to her friend John Ruskin:

There is going to be an exhibition for children at the Fine Art—the Private view is on Saturday—but I think it is very likely the children won't appreciate it. I often notice that they don't at all care for what grown-up people think they will.

Few adults have difficulty remembering their early favorites among children's books, but chances are no one else will have heard of them. My own were: *The Tale of Corally Crothers; Topsy Turvy and the Tin Clown; Bertram and His Marvelous Adventures,* by P. S. Gilbert, and *Háry János: The Obsitos* by Maud and Miska Petersham. Corally Crothers was a small girl "who had no sisters nor any brothers"—like me at the time I read her history—and rather moped about until she had the fine idea one day of running away from home. I recall Topsy Turvy only as a tomboy rag doll, but I loved Bertram dearly because he was burdened by the arrival of a brother, Baby Sam, at just about the same age—six—I acquired my own. Our feelings on the subject of smaller brothers were identical: negative. Bertram escaped from his troubles by meeting gorillas, bears and ibexes on his way home from school. I escaped from mine by reading about him. As for Hary Janos, he was vain, boastful and frivolous—about as flawed as I knew I was—yet he was redeemable and worthy of everyone's respect in the end. They all gave me some insight into myself and a sorely needed perspective on the wider world.

As adults, we should concern ourselves chiefly with exposing young children to a catholic variety of literary voices—commanding and diffident; fanciful and factual; comic and sober—asking only that the views they present be sane and spiritually truthful, that they open vistas of possibility rather than discourage lively curiosity. A child should have the opportunity to enjoy the nonsensical start of a romance in Edna Mitchell Preston's *Pop Corn and Ma Goodness*—

> Old Ma goes a-flying a-flippitty floppetty
> Old Pop takes a header a-dippitty doppetty
> They meet—oh their heads crack a-bippitty boppetty

—as well as to acquire wisdom from E. B. White's *Stuart Little*, who learns that it is possible, at one and the same time, to be "full of the joy of life and the fear of dogs." As grownups, our individual pictures of reality are so set that no book can materially alter their outlines or mood. But children are receptive to so wide a range of influence—so many mysteries and questions await clarification—that the books read and loved then are, in some inalterable way, woven into the fabric of their lives ever after.

Sarah Orne Jewett wrote, "The thing that teases the mind over and over for years, and at last gets itself put down rightly on paper—whether little or great, it belongs to Literature." From the child's point of view: that book which lingers in memory long years after he has heard or read it—little or great—belongs to Literature. Such a work, as Willa Cather described it, "must leave in the mind of the sensitive reader an intangible residuum of pleasure; a cadence, a quality of voice that is exclusively the writer's own, individual, unique. A quality that one can remember without the volume at hand, can experience over and over again in the mind but can never absolutely define, as one can experience in memory a melody, or the summer perfume of a garden. The magnitude of the subject is not of primary importance."

13: *When All the Sky Is Clear and Blue*

HE LIKED only blue and white skies," the wife of the printer Edmund Evans reminisced of Kate Greenaway. "Stormy effects gave her no pleasure." And in the same vein, Kate Greenaway once said of herself: "I wish there were no worms in the garden. I am so frightened when I sow things to see them turn up. I know they are useful, but they are not nice-looking."

To some degree, all who choose or write books for young children concur in this wish for "no worms in the garden." It is not that the authors of books for the young are cases of arrested development, nor that they are beings who close their eyes to life's deeper realities. But by the simple act of addressing themselves to children—or, truer perhaps, to the children they once were—they tacitly sidestep some of the most powerful emotional forces of adult life. Kenneth Grahame confirmed this fact when he spoke of what was to him the great charm of *The Wind in the Willows:* that "It is clean of the clash of sex." C. S. Lewis seems to voice a similar view when, in his collection of essays and stories *Of Other*

Worlds, he wrote of the Narnia books, "I am not quite sure what made me, in a particular year of my life, feel that not only a fairy tale, but a fairy tale addressed to children, was exactly what I must write—or burst. Partly, I think, that this art form permits, or compels, one to leave out things I wanted to leave out."

Though Lavinia Russ laments that with our rapidly changing mores it will not be another generation before "the sperm and the egg take the place of Mickey and Minnie Mouse," the eventuality does not seem likely. Just as most small children, in a reflex reaction, avert their eyes from "mushy" scenes in movies and on television, so too the authors of their tales instinctively shy away from the complexities and confusions of adult reality. Hear how George MacDonald handles a delicate matter between a king and his queen in *The Light Princess:*

> And the king said to himself, "All the queens of my acquaintance have children, some three, some seven, and some as many as twelve; and my queen has not one. I feel ill-used."

The queen sweetly smiles and replies, "You must have patience with a lady, you know, dear king."

Yet, times unquestionably have changed and with them our tolerance levels and attitudes. Both in his illustrations for *The Light Princess* and in his most recent fantasy, *In The Night Kitchen,* Maurice Sendak portrays two small children—a baby princess and a small boy dreamer—entirely in the nude, genitalia clearly evident and fantasy undiminished. Though it had never been done before, surely children were not the ones shocked by the innovation.

Edward Fenton noted perceptively in a 1968 piece for *Horn Book* that "Children's interests are as broad as the horizon. They are interested in practically everything—with the exception of sexual love, which bores them, being beyond their experience. They know that grownups fall in love and marry, but it is a convention they accept without caring about the details. As for all the other problems related to life (including death) it is impossible to overestimate the capacity of children to feel, suffer, understand and share them all if properly presented. But they must be in terms of action and plot.''

More than most contemporary authors for young children, Clyde Robert Bulla instinctively understands this thirst of children to learn about life from their stories. While his simple style and fast-moving plots make him the ideal writer for a child just beginning to read on his own, this simplicity is never achieved at the price of nuance lost or truth compromised. There are adults in his books who behave with shameless cruelty or venal self-interest, but Bulla never attempts to judge them. With a rare gift, he is able to paint character through revealing speech and incident. He does not tell his readers how life is, or how people are capable of behaving; he merely creates the situations that force his characters to be wholly themselves. His recent *The White Bird* is as subtle a story of the destructive power of misguided love as can be imagined, yet the author never once loses sight of the fact that he is, above all, a storyteller who must maintain his young reader's interest in a constantly developing tale.

When she won a prize for her first children's book, *Tell Me a Mitzi,* Lore Segal confided, ''The next book I do I would like really to be strictly for children, written from the child's viewpoint. This one was for me.'' But surely the best of authors and illustrators must always work in large part ''for me.'' Beatrix Potter's little books give small children the pleasure they do, not

BEATRIX POTTER *The Tale of Mrs. Tiggy Winkle*

because they are childlike in their view, but because they are so thoroughly sensible and wholly forthright about the realities with which they deal. From story to story, the tales mesh in countless small ways that only a mature and thoroughly engaged mind —one working "for me"—could conceive and control. The hedgehog-laundress heroine of *The Tale of Mrs. Tiggy Winkle* washes the very handkerchief that Benjamin Bunny used in *his* tale to carry off Mr. McGregor's onions. In *Ginger and Pickles*, the two doll customers—Lucinda and Jane—are the co-owners of the dollhouse in *The Tale of Two Bad Mice*. A palpable reality, as solid as the world's, was created by Miss Potter from the elements of her various animal adventures. And those larger truths that she encounters in her tales are never sidestepped. Of the pigs in one of her books, she wrote: "They led prosperous uneventful lives and their end was bacon," an inescapable truth that was later to provide the dramatic core for E. B. White's *Charlotte's Web*. Children can be pitiless realists when supplied with simple, nononsense facts.

Yet, this said, it is difficult to set the reasonable level of anxi-

ety and stress in children's books, particularly those for the very
young. Not long ago, a college-age friend was recalling a book
that disturbed her as a small child. It was about a horse who lost
a leg, she recalled, "And I just couldn't say to myself, as I might
now, 'That's O.K., I know it's likely to all come right in the end.'
The suffering caused me genuine pain and I never liked to hear
the story because of it." Though children may be, on the one
hand, tough-minded and resilient, accepting unblinkingly many a
harsh reality that does not immediately touch their lives, they are
curiously vulnerable to other situations that are scarcely comprehensible to an adult reader.

A nursery-school teacher has told me of reading William
Steig's *Sylvester and the Magic Pebble* to herself before trying it
in class. "I found it boring," particularly that long part where
Sylvester disappears [having turned himself into a stone] and his
parents carry on for so many pages trying to find out where he has
gone." Yet, it was that very section which held her class of four-
year-olds transfixed. "When I closed that book," she reported,
"I realized for the first time how much small children must worry
about being lost and whether their parents will really care enough
to come looking. They found the story tremendously reassuring."

What is perhaps also reassuring for children in *Sylvester* is
that his story represents a kind of metaphor for resurrection.
Transformed into an unfeeling stone by a bit of misapplied magic,
he can neither move nor speak—as dead as any child can imagine
being. Yet his parents are miraculously able to restore him. In the
literature of childhood, adults and children alike can find temporary refuge from the power of death. In the play *Rosencrantz
and Guildenstern Are Dead* by Tom Stoppard, the loquacious
Rosencrantz wonders: "Whatever became of the moment when

GARTH WILLIAMS *Charlotte's Web*

one first knew about death? There must have been one, a moment in childhood when it first occurred to you that you don't go on forever. It must have been shattering—stamped into one's memory. And yet I can't remember it. It never occurred to me at all. What does one make of that? We must be born with an intuition of mortality.''

In E. B. White's *Charlotte's Web,* of course, that moment is unforgettably recorded when the young Wilbur learns from a wise old sheep what his fate is to be.

''You know why they're fattening you up, don't you?''
''No,'' said Wilbur.
''Well, I don't like to spread bad news,'' said the sheep,

"but they're fattening you up because they're going to kill you, that's why."

"They're going to *what?*" screamed Wilbur. Fern grew rigid on her stool.

"Kill you. Turn you into smoked bacon and ham," continued the old sheep. "Almost all young pigs get murdered by the farmer as soon as the real cold weather sets in . . ."

"Stop!" screamed Wilbur. "I don't want to die! Save me, somebody! Save me!"

I can remember driving with my father as a small girl and his singing to keep me entertained. One of his favorite songs— and one I always dreaded hearing—was "I'm Forever Blowing Bubbles." I am sure he felt it was a singularly appropriate selection, but whenever he came to the lines:

> They fly so high,
> nearly reach the sky.
> Then like my dreams
> they fade and die . . .

tears always filled my eyes. They seemed to me the saddest lines in all the world, though I never understood why. They had somehow wakened that "intuition of mortality" which childhood and much of its literature usually conceal so successfully.

We all of us know perfectly well that the skies of childhood outside of romantic literature are anything but clear and blue for long stretches of time for all children. Yet, in looking back on its best moments—in life and in the books we remember—it is probably as close as any of us ever come to pure joy, to innocence and to a belief in our own immortality. The most hard-headed adult

finds it difficult not to respond to Nathaniel Hawthorne's sentimental salute at the close of one of his *Twice Told Tales:*

> Sweet has been the charm of childhood on my spirit. . . . As
> the pure breath of children revives the life of aged men, so is
> our moral nature revived by their free and simple thoughts,
> their native feeling, their airy mirth, for little cause or none,
> their grief, soon roused and soon allayed. Their influence on
> us is at least reciprocal with ours on them. When our infancy
> is almost forgotten, and our boyhood long departed, though it
> seems but as yesterday; when life settles darkly down upon
> us, and we doubt whether to call ourselves young any more,
> then it is good to steal away from the society of bearded men,
> and even of gentler women, and spend an hour or two with
> children. After drinking from those fountains of still fresh
> existence, we shall return into the crowd, as I do now, to strug-
> gle onward and do our part in life, perhaps as fervently as
> ever, but, for a time, with a kinder and purer heart, and a
> spirit more lightly wise.

In the best of children's books, too, we find this quality of
spiritual refreshment, of things seen simply and savored truly as
they might have been on the first day of creation.

Appendix: Voices of Quality
An Idiosyncratic Book List

We have a world for each one, but we do not have a world for all.

ANTONIO PORCHIA, Voices

Anyone who presumes to suggest "the best books" for children in a land where some 35,000 juvenile titles are currently in print and new books continue to appear at the rate of more than 2,000 each year knows that he can please few except that handful of parents, aunts, uncles, grandmothers, grandfathers and disinterested lovers of children's books who, by luck, in consulting his selection may match the right book and child. In a field where each season brings a crop of new titles similar to, if not indistinguishable from, last year's and the year's before that, the built-in obsolescence of the average book for small children may surpass that of the American automobile.

The list that follows is limited to books for children from two to seven, the span of years during which they are most at an adult's mercy as to the choice of the books that reach them and, at the same time, the period during which they are most receptive to the few books that speak to them alone. The titles were, for the most part, selected from the large number of books I have reviewed over the past five years for the late New York *Herald Tribune*'s *Book Week, The New York Times Book Review* and the *Chicago Tribune*'s and *Washington Post*'s *Book World*. Other choices were the result of happy visits to the local library's children's room both for and with my children since 1963. Those books with publication dates prior to 1966 were still in print late in 1970. Such obvious choices as Beatrix Potter's *The Tale of Peter Rabbit* or *The Tale of Two Bad Mice,* standbys like *Make Way for Ducklings* and even more recent titles by popular authors and illustrators are left out because they are so well known, their reputations precede them and the child will have ample opportunity to read or hear them. Most of the titles that follow have not yet weathered the sometimes quixotic test of time, but nonetheless deserve to be known by a wide audience of present-day children.

The list is primarily for those not infrequent occasions when one wants to find just the right birthday present or get-well gift for a special child, or when one simply must have a book on a particular subject for a particular child right now and has little time for in-depth research. Where titles are listed by specific subject matter rather than age grouping, I have tried to arrange selections in ascending order of age, youngest listeners (age two) up to oldest (age seven). But, as J. R. R. Tolkien noted of all worthwhile reading fare for children, "Their books like their clothes should allow for growth, and their books at any rate should encourage it." The age level, therefore, beyond those books specified for youngest children, need not be interpreted too strictly. A younger child will reach to grasp subject matter of special interest to him.

It should be borne in mind, too, that not all gift books need be between hard covers. Happily, the list of good children's books in paperback grows each year, even in the picture-book category, and the quality of their manufacture improves as well. From England, *A Puffin Book of Verse,* the more recent *A Young Puffin Book of Verse* and *The Puffin Book of Nursery Rhymes* make excellent house gifts to families with small children, as do Schocken Books' *English Fairy Tales* and *More English Fairy Tales,* collected by Joseph Jacobs, and the twelve "color" *Fairy Books* (from *Blue* through *Crimson* and *Lilac* to *Yellow*) of Andrew Lang, offered in sturdy paper editions by Dover.

The categories chosen for special groupings have proved useful on a variety of occasions with my own children.

As a guide for use on trips to the library, however, the list may prove to be more frustrating than useful, since it is often difficult, with

213

the constant traffic in most children's-book rooms, to find a given title on the shelves. The librarian who knows the ebb and flow of her own branch's titles can be far more helpful, as can ten minutes spent browsing on a low stool, seeking out unknown treasures on one's own. The library visitor might keep in mind that certain picture-book artists and authors can almost always be counted on to entertain. A list of such sure-fire staples should include: Edward Ardizzone, Eric Blegvad, Clyde Robert Bulla, André François, Paul Galdone, M. B. Goffstein, Arnold Lobel, Anita Lobel, Leo Lionni, Bruno Munari, Ann Kirn, Bill Peet, Maurice Sendak, Dr. Seuss, Tomi Ungerer, Margot Zemach and Uri Shulevitz.

Last, it should be emphasized that the lists which follow are by no means all-inclusive in their categories. What can be said without qualification is that every title which appears has been read by the list maker and pleased her and/or two reasonably discriminating children, that all offer surprises and rewards beyond the run-of-the-mill, and that each is a voice of quality. The spirit in which the list has been compiled was best described by Lavinia Russ, long-time director of the children's-book department for The Scribner Book Store in New York and later children's-book editor of *Publishers' Weekly,* when she observed: "Anyone who loves a child and a book wants to get them together."

Not every book, of course, on this or any other list can or should please every child. When building any child's personal library, it is always chastening to bear in mind the words of Beatrix Potter to her biographer, Margaret Lane: "When I was a little girl, I was satisfied with about six books. . . . I think that children now have too many."

FOR THE HOME LIBRARY

The Mother Goose Treasury. Illustrated by Raymond Briggs. Coward-McCann, 1966.
    408 well-chosen rhymes from Peter and Iona Opie's compendium, accompanied by 897 lively illustrations, most in bold color.

A Child's Book of Poems. Illustrated by Gyo Fujikawa. Grosset and
Dunlap, 1969.
A varied anthology containing selections from William Blake and
Emily Dickinson as well as folk-song excerpts and anonymous non-
sense. A cheerful, sensitively illustrated first book of poetry.

Lullabies and Night Songs. William Engvick, editor. Music by Alec
Wilder. Illustrated by Maurice Sendak. Harper & Row, 1965.
Verse by Eleanor Farjeon, James Thurber, the editor and others set
to original music in most cases. More familiar lullabies get pleasing
new arrangements.

Grimm's Fairy Tales. Introduction by Frances Clarke Sayers. Paintings
in color by children of fifteen nations. Follett, 1968.
Fifty Grimm tales in which words take precedence over illustration.
The paintings—one to a story—will encourage children to try some
of their own.

The Best Word Book Ever. By Richard Scarry. Golden, 1963. Or one of
Mr. Scarry's later, similar picture encyclopedias: *The Storybook Dic-
tionary* (Golden) or *What Do People Do All Day?* (Random House).
These lively primers of the workaday world, filled with a bustling
animal citizenry, are virtually guaranteed to please children from
two-and-a-half to five.

FIRST BOOKS

Things to See: A Child's World of Familiar Objects. Photographed in
color by Thomas Matthiesen. Platt & Munk, 1966.

A B C: An Alphabet Book. Photographed in color by Thomas Matthiesen.
Platt & Munk, 1968.
Each is a pleasing collection of just enough objects, well photographed
to hold a small viewer's attention for a sitting.

ABC. By John Burningham. Bobbs-Merrill, 1967.
Bold and droll illustration of objects sure to delight.

The Baby Animal ABC. Illustrated by Robert Broomfield. Picture Puffin (paper), 1969.

Simple, satisfying illustrations of animals and their young.

Old MacDonald. Illustrated by Mel Crawford. Golden, 1967.

Large, pleasing pictures of farm animals which look real enough to pat accompany the familiar song.

Which Way to the Zoo? By William Wondriska. Holt, Rinehart & Winston, 1962.

In which a small child learns the names of lots of wild animals via an engaging plot device.

Bears are Sleeping. Words and music by Yulya. Pictures by Nonny Hogrogian. Scribner, 1967.

A lilting Russian lullaby for wintry evenings.

The Good Bird. By Peter Wezel. Harper & Row, 1966.

The Naughty Bird. By Peter Wezel. Follett, 1967.

Two wordless tales of different birds, the engaging, outsize illustrations sufficient to tell all.

Brian Wildsmith's Wild Animals. By Brian Wildsmith. Watts, 1967.

Brian Wildsmith's Fishes. By Brian Wildsmith. Watts, 1968.

Full-page, rainbow-palette renditions of familiar wild animals and less familiar sea inhabitants.

AGES TWO TO THREE

Celestino Piatti's Animal ABC. By John Reid. Illustrated by Celestino Piatti. Atheneum, 1966.

Handsomely designed and illustrated, and possibly the only alphabet with Xopiatti for X.

The Elephant and the Bad Baby. By Elfrida Vipont. Illustrated by Raymond Briggs. Coward-McCann, 1970.

The importance of ''please'' is firmly established in this winning tale of a bad baby's adventures.

If I Were a Mother. By Kazue Mizumura. Crowell, 1968.

A tender primer of animal mothers and offspring beautifully illustrated.

The Moon in My Room. By Uri Shulevitz. Harper & Row, 1963.

A reassuring fantasy about what happens in a small boy's moonlit room.

Push Kitty. By Jan Wahl. Illustrated by Garth Williams. Harper & Row, 1968.

An unwilling kitten is forced to play baby—up to a point. Droll.

Robin in Red Boots. By Heinz Herzka. Illustrated by Heiri Steiner. Harcourt Brace Jovanovich, 1970.

A small girl's fantasy adventures (six) as she takes her first steps alone into the wide world. Beguiling illustrations.

Sleepy People. By M. B. Goffstein. Farrar, Straus & Giroux, 1966.

Four sleepy little people yawn, stretch, drink warm drinks and put everyone in the mood for bed.

The Comic Adventures of Old Mother Hubbard and Her Dog. Illustrated by Arnold Lobel. Bradbury, 1968.

A pleasing low-key rendition of the high-spirited rhyme.

Rewarding pictorial details encourage frequent re-examination.

The Gingerbread Boy. Illustrated by William Curtis Holdsworth. Farrar, Straus & Giroux, 1968.

A chaste telling of a favorite tale in sepia with an oddly compelling purity.

The Owl and the Pussy-Cat. By Edward Lear. Illustrated by William Pene Du Bois. Doubleday, 1961.

Perfect illustrations to accompany this favorite childhood ballad.

AGES THREE TO FIVE

Across the Sea. By M. B. Goffstein. Farrar, Straus & Giroux, 1968.

A pleasing trio of modern folk tales, in which ''Sophie's Picnic'' is a memorable celebration of life's simple joys.

Add-a-Line Alphabet. By Don Freeman. Golden Gate, 1968.

An alphabet book which encourages active participation by the viewer.

A Child's Calendar. By John Updike. Illustrated by Nancy Ekholm Burkert. Knopf, 1965.

Rhymes on seasonal variations and moods filled with humor, wit and true poetry.

Corduroy. By Don Freeman. Viking, 1968.

How a small black girl finds the perfect brown Teddy.

Elephant Boy. By William Kotzwinkle. Illustrated by Joe Servello. Farrar, Straus & Giroux, 1970.

A tour-de-force visit with earliest man that gives the feeling of what life must have been like then.

Frederick. By Leo Lionni. Pantheon, 1966.

What poets give to the world, eloquently told and illustrated.

From King Boggen's Hall to Nothing-At-All. By Blair Lent. Atlantic–Little, Brown, 1967.

A mind-expanding collection of improbable dwellings found in traditional rhymes and limericks.

The Great Blueness and Other Predicaments. By Arnold Lobel. Harper & Row, 1968.

A winning flight of fancy on how the world came to be multi-colored.

Hector Protector and As I Went Over the Water. Two nursery rhymes with pictures by Maurice Sendak. Harper & Row, 1965.

A delightful third dimension to Mother Goose via the illustrator's inspired conception and improvised dialogue.

Henry Explores the Jungle. By Mark Taylor. Illustrated by Graham Booth. Atheneum, 1968.

A junior explorer crosses wildest suburbia and finds a real-life tiger.

I Packed My Trunk. By Barbara K. Walker. Illustrated by Carl Kock. Follet, 1969.

In which 26 alphabetized items, occasionally quite unlikely ones, are stuffed into a trunk.

Mommy, Buy Me a China Doll. Ozark folk song adapted by Harve Zemach. Illustrated by Margot Zemach. Follett, 1966.

A spirited children's song set to perfect pictures.

218

Mr. Miacca. An English folk tale. Illustrated by Evaline Ness. Holt, Rinehart & Winston, 1967.

A charmingly scary tale about a bumbling London bogeyman.

Noah's Ark. By William Wiesner. Dutton, 1966.

The Tower of Babel. By William Wiesner. Viking, 1968.

Biblical tales faithfully and gracefully simplified with compelling "funny-paper"-style illustration.

Oh Lord, I Wish I Was a Buzzard. By Polly Greenberg. Illustrated by Aliki. Macmillan, 1968.

A touching, non-sentimental look at a small black cotton picker of the not necessarily distant past.

One Monday Morning. By Uri Shulevitz. Scribner, 1967.

A fantasy in which a royal family visits a small boy in his city tenement.

One Wide River to Cross. Folk song adapted by Barbara Emberley. Illustrated by Ed Emberley. Prentice-Hall, 1966.

A witty, graphically sophisticated counting book on the Noah's Ark theme.

Penny. By Beatrice Schenk de Regniers. Illustrated by Marvin Bileck. Viking, 1966.

A girl no bigger than a penny finds a home, family, mate and high adventure.

Raminagrobis and the Mice. By Harold Berson. Seabury, 1965.

In which a diabolical cat meets his match and more, illustrated with an incisive pen.

AGES FOUR TO SEVEN

Brer Rabbit and His Tricks. By Ennis Rees. Illustrated by Edward Gorey. Scott, 1967.

More of Brer Rabbit's Tricks. By Ennis Rees. Illustrated by Edward Gorey. Scott, 1968.

A lively retelling of tales in colloquial, non-dialect verse.

Clotilda. By Jack Kent. Random House, 1969.

A funny book about what happens when a non-believer in fairies meets one.

Charlie and the Chocolate Factory. By Roald Dahl. Illustrated by Joseph Schindelman. Knopf, 1964.

A small boy wins the chance to see the inside of Mr. Wonka's fabulous factory, a rare treat for readers of all ages.

The Four Clever Brothers. The Grimm Brothers' tale. Illustrated by Felix Hoffmann. Harcourt Brace Jovanovich, 1967.

An absorbing story of four brothers, their special gifts and adventures.

Gertrude's Child. By Richard Hughes. Illustrated by Rick Schreiter. Quist, 1966.

A tale set in a topsy-turvy world where toys possess children.

Harriet and the Promised Land. By Jacob Lawrence. Windmill/Simon & Schuster, 1968.

An epic conception of both story and artwork in this tale of Harriet Tubman, who led more than 300 fellow slaves to freedom.

Hurrah, We're Outward Bound. By Peter Spier. Doubleday, 1968.

One of the virtuoso illustrator's Mother Goose Library volumes: this one a collection of sea rhymes and chanteys accompanied by authentic nineteenth-century sailing ships.

Mazel and Shlimazel or the Milk of a Lioness. By Isaac Bashevis Singer. Illustrated by Margot Zemach. Farrar, Straus & Giroux, 1967.

How Good Luck and Bad battle over the fate of a simple village boy, Tam.

Mr. Brown and Mr. Gray. By William Wondriska. Holt, Rinehart & Winston, 1968.

Two pigs inadvertently stumble on the answer to ''What Is Happiness?'' in a wondrous wise tale.

The Old Nurse's Stocking Basket. By Eleanor Farjeon. Illustrated by Edward Ardizzone. Walck, 1965.

An old nurse spins beguiling fairy tales to match the size of the hole in the child's stocking she is mending.

Sam, Bangs and Moonshine. By Evaline Ness. Holt, Rinehart & Winston, 1966.

A small girl learns to distinguish between truth and ''moonshine'' when she narrowly misses causing a real-life tragedy.

The Swineherd. The Andersen tale. Illustrated by Erik Blegvad. Harcourt Brace Jovanovich, 1958.

In which a spoiled princess gets not a prince but her just deserts.

Some of the Days of Everett Anderson. By Lucille Clifton. Illustrated by Evaline Ness. Holt, Rinehart & Winston, 1970.

Light verse on a small (six-year-old) black boy's awareness of himself and the city world around him.

To Be a Slave. By Julius Lester. Dial, 1968.

First-hand accounts of slavery given continuity by the author's unobtrusive narrative bridges. ''I wanted the material to speak for itself,'' Lester has said. ''I was Virgil leading you through hell.''

The Twelve Dancing Princesses. The Grimm Brothers' tale. Translated by Elizabeth Shub. Illustrated by Uri Shulevitz. Scribner, 1966.

An elegant *art nouveau* rendition of this magical fairy tale.

SOME SUPERIOR BOOKS IN SERIES

FOR AGES THREE TO FIVE

Little Bear, etc. By Else Holmelund Minarik. Illustrated by Maurice Sendak. Harper & Row, 1957 & on.

The trials and triumphs of a little bear growing bigger, in five volumes.

Bedtime for Frances, etc. By Russell Hoban. Illustrated by Lillian Hoban. Harper & Row, 1960 & on.

In which a badger girl-child suffers from and overcomes many a childhood trauma: food fetishes, nighttime fears, a new baby sister, etc.

The Story of Babar, etc. By Jean de Brunhoff. Random House, 1933 & on.

The adventures of a thoroughly French elephant, his family and friends, a dynasty now into its second generation continued by the author-illustrator's son, Laurent.

The Mellops Go Flying, etc. By Tomi Ungerer. Harper & Row, 1957 & on.
An irrepressible pig family's lively encounters with near disaster.

FOR AGES FOUR TO SEVEN

Little Tim and the Brave Sea Captain, etc. By Edward Ardizzone. Walck, 1955 & on.
Life on the bounding main as experienced by Little Tim and assorted friends, including a stowaway dog.

Curious George, etc. By Hans A. Rey. Houghton Mifflin, 1941 & on.
A mischievous monkey rushes from one misadventure to the next, impelled always by his insatiable curiosity.

Kap the Kappa, etc. By Betty Jean Lifton. Illustrated by Eiichi Mitsui. Morrow, 1960 & on.
These magical escapades of a Japanese water sprite are gripping.

The House on East 88th Street, etc. By Bernard Waber. Houghton Mifflin, 1962 & on.
What happens to a pet crocodile living with a family in a New York City brownstone.

The Cat Club, etc. By Esther Averill. Harper & Row, 1944 & on.
The droll adventures of Jenny Linsky, a Greenwich Village cat, and her feline compatriots.

SICKBED SPECIALS

Babar's Trunk. By Jean de Brunhoff. Random House, 1969. Two and up.
Four little books in their own trunk make a fine introduction to Babar's brood—on a picnic, skiing, in the garden and by the sea.

The Terrible Tiger. By Jack Prelutsky. Illustrated by Arnold Lobel. Macmillan, 1970. Two and up.
A truly terrible tiger fulfills the child's worst fears and goes merrily on his way to more truly terrible adventures.

The Nutshell Library. By Maurice Sendak. Harper & Row, 1962. Three and up.

Another tiny foursome (also available singly in larger size): *Alligators All Around,* an alphabet; *One Was Johnny,* a counting book; *Chicken Soup with Rice,* a cozy book of months; and *Pierre: A Cautionary Tale,* about a boy who always says "I don't care!"

Famous Sally. By Shirley Jackson. Illustrated by Charles Slackman. Quist, 1966. Three and up.

Fantasy adventures of a little girl who wants desperately to be somebody.

The Slant Book. By Peter Newell. Tuttle, 1967. Three and up.

A delight first published in 1910, this doggerel adventure of a runaway baby carriage (baby inside) is guaranteed to please. Its slanted pages contribute greatly to the sense of impending doom.

Tell Me a Mitzi. By Lore Segal. Illustrated by Harriet Pincus. Farrar, Straus & Giroux, 1970. Three and up.

A cozy trio of tales about Mitzi and her baby brother, Jacob—one of them a sneezy, sick-in-bed tale.

The Wedding Procession of the Rag Doll and the Broom Handle, and Who Was in It. By Carl Sandburg. Illustrated by Harriet Pincus. Harcourt Brace Jovanovich, 1967. Three and up.

A beautifully conceived world for a little-known Sandburg child's tale.

Catfish. By Edith and Clement Hurd. Viking, 1970. Four and up.

A wild and funny story about the fastest cat on wheels.

Ed Emberley's Drawing Book of Animals. By Ed Emberley. Little, Brown, 1970. Four and up.

Guaranteed to have any child who can make lines, squares and circles drawing marvelous animals on his own.

My Book About Me. By Dr. Seuss and Roy McKie. Random House, 1969. Four and up.

The child collaborates in writing his own biography full of pertinent and impertinent information.

Farewell to Shady Glade. By Bill Peet. Houghton Mifflin, 1966. Four and up.

A winning tale about sixteen assorted woodland animals evicted from their paradise by a bulldozer. Rachel Carson would have liked it.

The Gillygoofang. By George Mendoza. Illustrated by Mercer Mayer. Dial, 1968.

Inspired nonsense about a fish that swims backward to keep the water out of its eyes.

The Hat. By Tomi Ungerer. Parents' Magazine Press, 1970.

An antic adventure of a magic hat and its fortunate wearer.

Joco and the Fishbone. By William Wiesner. Viking, 1966.

A felicitous adaptation of an Arabian Nights tale about a hunchback who swallows a fishbone, dies and, miraculously, is returned to life.

Johnny Lion's Bad Day. By Edith and Clement Hurd. Harper & Row, 1970. Four and up.

An I-Can-Read Book about a small boy lion who is feverish and in bed.

The Adventures of Paddy Pork. By John Goodall. Harcourt Brace Jovanovich, 1968.

The Ballooning Adventures of Paddy Pork. By John Goodall. Harcourt Brace Jovanovich, 1969. Three and up.

Two silent adventures with ingenious half-page inserts that create moving pictures.

That Mean Man. By Liesel Moak Skorpen. Illustrated by Emily McCully. Harper & Row, 1968. Four and up.

About the meanest man in the world, his dreadful wife and terrible children.

MANNERS

What Do You Say, Dear? By Sesyle Joslin. Illustrated by Maurice Sendak. Scott, 1958.

What Do You Do, Dear? By Sesyle Joslin. Illustrated by Maurice Sendak.
Scott, 1961.
The proper things to do and say in a number of wildly improbable
situations slyly prepare children for tamer social occasions.
The Goops and How to Be Them: A Manual of Manners for Polite Infants.
By Gelett Burgess. Dover (paper), 1968.
*More Goops and How Not to Be Them: A Manual of Manners for Impolite
Infants.* By Gelett Burgess. Dover (paper), 1968.
Manners for polite and impolite infants, as pertinent and droll now
as when first published in 1903.

FAMILY LIFE

The Sorely Trying Day. By Russell and Lillian Hoban. Harper & Row,
1964.
A Victorian setting for familiar family trials.
The Quarreling Book. By Charlotte Zolotow. Illustrated by Arnold Lobel.
Harper & Row, 1963.
A rainy day goes from bad to worse after Father forgets to kiss
Mother goodbye.
Mommies at Work. By Eve Merriam. Illustrated by Beni Montresor.
Knopf, 1961.
Up women's liberation! Mommies build bridges as well as bake cakes.
I'd Rather Stay with You. By Charlotte Steiner. Seabury, 1965.
A baby kangaroo is coaxed, wheedled and persuaded to leave his
mother's pouch.
Friday Night Is Papa Night. By Ruth Sonneborn. Illustrated by Emily
McCully. Viking, 1970.
A hard-working Puerto Rican father, away all week, receives a hero's
welcome.
Angry Kate. By Elizabeth Janeway. Illustrated by Charles Slackman.
Harper & Row, 1963.
A thoroughly bad girl is banished to an unlikely new home, the zoo.

Throw a Kiss, Harry. By Mary Chalmers. Harper & Row, 1958.

Take a Nap, Harry. By Mary Chalmers. Harper & Row, 1964.

Be Good, Harry. By Mary Chalmers. Harper & Row, 1967.

Three tiny delights about a kitten offspring with a mind of his own.

SIBLING RIVALRY

Peter's Chair. By Ezra Jack Keats. Harper & Row, 1967.

In which a brother reluctantly accepts a new baby sister, but not without a fight.

A Baby Sister for Frances. By Russell and Lillian Hoban. Harper & Row, 1964.

A small girl badger no longer feels loved when Gloria arrives.

I'll Fix Anthony. By Judith Viorst. Illustrated by Arnold Lobel. Harper & Row, 1969.

A younger brother plans the revenge he will take when he is six.

Tom in the Middle. By Berthe Amoss. Harper & Row, 1968.

The trials of a sibling middleman lovingly observed.

A Birthday for Frances. By Russell and Lillian Hoban. Harper & Row, 1968.

"Your birthday is always the one that is not now," complains an older sister of the fuss being made over Gloria's natal day.

Harvey's Hideout. By Russell and Lillian Hoban. Parents' Magazine Press, 1969.

"That is just what I would expect from a selfish, inconsiderate, stupid, no good little brother like you," says Mildred, and sibling relations deteriorate from there.

Stevie. By John Steptoe. Harper & Row, 1969.

In which an older black boy resents and finally comes to like a temporary foster brother—a convincing slice of city life lovingly pictured and colloquially told.

AESTHETICS—IMAGINATION STRETCHERS

Topsy-Turvies. By Mitsumasa Anno. Walker-Weatherhill, 1970. Three and up.
    Optically ambiguous and thoroughly entrancing pictures suggest new worlds of visual possibility.
Journeys of Sebastian. By Fernando Krahn. Delacorte, 1968. Four and up.
    The mind-expanding fantasy adventures of a small, soulful hero—riding inside a bee, walking to the other side of a mirror, discovering a fantastic beast. Wordless and eloquent.
Goldie the Dollmaker. By M. B. Goffstein. Farrar, Straus & Giroux, 1969. Five and up.
    In which the artist's life becomes comprehensible via a simple and moving fable.
The Many Ways of Seeing. By Janet Gaylord Moore. World, 1968. Nine and up.
    No book on art appreciation is less stuffy nor more perceptive than this 141-page volume by an associate curator at the Cleveland Museum. For parents and children.

FOR BUDDING NATURALISTS

Children of the Forest. Verse and pictures by Elsa Beskow. Delacorte, 1969. Two to four.
    A Swedish favorite about life among the woodland elves. Lovingly illustrated.
When the Root Children Wake Up. By Helen D. Fish. Illustrated by Sibylle V. Olfers. Lippincott, 1941. Two to four.
    A fanciful tale about seasonal changes in a real woodland.
The Fireflies. By Max Bolliger. Illustrated by Jiří Trnka. Atheneum, 1970. Three to six.

In which the life cycle of living things is nicely conveyed in a suspenseful tale about firefly people.

Fox and the Fire. By Miska Miles. Illustrated by John Schoenherr. Little, Brown, 1966. Four and up.

A fox-eye view of making one's way in the world by a team that seldom misses on nature subjects. (*Rabbit Garden* [Little, Brown, 1967] is equally successful.)

Little Apes. By Gladys Conklin. Illustrated by Joseph Cellini. Holiday House, 1970. Four to seven.

Well-drawn baby chimpanzees, gorillas, orangutans and gibbons make clear family differences.

ANTI-WAR BOOKS

The Two Giants. By Michael Foreman. Pantheon, 1967. Two and up.
How two collossi fall out, giant-hug and make up.

Potatoes, Potatoes. By Anita Lobel. Harper & Row, 1967. Three and up.
Even generals are somebody's children and their mothers don't like them playing with guns.

The Duck in the Gun. By Joy Cowley. Illustrated by Edward Sorel. Doubleday, 1969. Four and up.
How a nesting duck gives an army time to discover the pleasures of peace.

How the Children Stopped the Wars. By Jan Wahl. Illustrated by Mitchell Miller. Farrar, Straus & Giroux, 1969. Four and up.
A children's crusade led by a shepherd boy succeeds in its mission.

Return to Hiroshima. By Betty Jean Lifton. Photographs by Eikoh Hosoe. Atheneum, 1970. Six and up.
Low-key text and photographs combine to tell it as it was, is and will be for the survivors of Hiroshima. A whisper more eloquent than most shouts against war.

ON OLD AGE

Maxie. By Mildred Kantrowitz. Illustrated by Emily McCully. Parents' Magazine Press, 1970. Four and up.
The life of a lonely old lady made wholly absorbing, sympathetic and meaningful.

ON DEATH

Cock Robin. By Barbara Cooney. Scribner, 1965. Three and up.
Great joy and deep sorrow chronicled by a winning woodland citizenry, matter-of-factly and reassuringly.
The Dead Bird. By Margaret Wise Brown. Illustrated by Remy Charlip. Scott, 1958.
What happens when some small children find a bird "cold dead and stone still with no heart beating." The sense of loss and the triumph of life's continuity are beautifully balanced.
Sir Ribbeck of Ribbeck of Havelland. By Theodor Fontane. Illustrated by Nonny Hogrogian. Macmillan, 1969.
A reassuring tale of the fruitful old age of Sir Ribbeck and how, on his death, his good deeds live on after him.

SEEING THE WORLD

This Is London (or Paris, Rome, Munich, New York, etc.). By M. Sasek. Macmillan, 1959 and on. Three and up.
The Michelin guides for the under-seven set.
The Brave Little Goat of Monsieur Seguin. By Alphonse Daudet. Illustrated by Chiyoko Nakatani. World, 1968. Four and up.
A loving glimpse of Provence in a bittersweet tale.
A Village in Normandy. By Laurence. Bobbs-Merrill, 1968. Three and up.

229

In which a French village becomes home as a postman is followed on his daily rounds.

WOULD-BE ENGINEERS, ASTRONAUTS, ETC.

Journey to the Moon. By Erich Fuchs. Delacorte, 1970. Three and up.
  In which moon flights are made comprehensible in explicit yet poetic illustration. All text (two pages) precedes the wordless flight.
The Giant Book of Things in Space. By George Zaffo. Doubleday, 1969.
  The nursery set's *2001.*
The ABC of Cars, Trucks and Machines. By Adelaide Hall. Illustrated by William Dugan. American Heritage, 1970. Three to six.
  All the aficionado might want to know about things that go, clearly and appealingly illustrated.

FOR SHY CHILDREN

The Shy Little Girl. By Phyllis Krasilovsky. Illustrated by Trina Schart-Hyman. Little, Brown, 1970. Five to eight.
  Reassurance that the problem is surmountable.
Benjie. By Joan Lexau. Illustrated by Don Bolognese. Dial, 1964.
  How a little boy living with his grandmother in Harlem discovers he can speak when he must. (*Benjie on His Own* [1970] shows how far Benjie has advanced.)

FOR THE CHILD WHO MUST GET GLASSES

Spectacles. By Ellen Raskin. Atheneum, 1968.
  About Iris Fogel, who makes hilarious visual *faux pas* because she can't see.

FOR THE OVERWEIGHT CHILD

The Fattest Bear in the First Grade. By Barbara Robinson. Illustrated by
Cyndy Szekeres. Random House, 1969.
The rewards of being thin, the trials of being fat told in a droll tale
about a portly koala bear, Roberta.

NOTABLE RECENT TITLES

Gobble Grown Grunt. By Peter Spier. Doubleday, 1971.
A compelling compendium of some 600 animals, together with the bleats,
croaks, squeaks and squawks appropriate to each.
Count and See. By Tana Hoban. Macmillan, 1972.
A consummately intelligent counting book that goes from 1 hydrant to
100 peas in 10 pods via simple words and handsome black-and-white
photographs.
The Piggy in the Puddle. By Charlotte Pomerantz. Illustrated by James
Marshall. Macmillan, 1974.
About a family of pigs and one stubborn offspring who won't be lured
from the middle of a delectably squishy puddle.
Father Fox's Pennyrhymes. By Clyde Watson. Illustrated by Wendy Wat-
son. Crowell, 1971.
An authentically colloquial, breezily illustrated collection of zany new
American nursery rhymes.
Mittens for Kittens. And other Rhymes about Cats. Selected by Leonore
Blegvad. Illustrated by Eric Blegvad. Atheneum, 1974.
A varied potpourri of old English verse about cats, some familiar, some
seeming fresh minted. The color work is masterly.
The Princess and Froggie. By Harve and Kaethe Zemach. Illustrated by
Margot Zemach. Farrar, Straus & Giroux, 1975.
Three beguiling little tales about a small, lumpy princess and her froggie
friend who helps her out of every tear-provoking crisis.
No Kiss for Mother. By Tomi Ungerer. Harper & Row, 1973.

In which a spoiled-rotten kitten, Piper Paw, revolts against parental and all other authority. The black humor scores several telling points about adult-child relationships.

Farmer Palmer's Wagon Ride. By William Steig. Farrar, Straus & Giroux, 1974.

A disarmingly sweet tale about friendship and the things in life that really count, from a writer/artist who knows.

Frog and Toad Together. By Arnold Lobel. Harper & Row, 1972.

Delightful ups and downs of two splay-footed friends who are mostly tolerant of each other's peccadilloes.

The Church Mice and the Moon. By Graham Oakley. Atheneum, 1974.

Inspired comedy about two captive mice who give some muddleheaded scientists a run for their misguided notions during a supposed trip to the moon.

Baby. By Fran Manushkin. Illustrated by Ronald Himmler. Harper & Row, 1973.

In which Mrs. Tracy's baby, wise beyond its 8-plus months *in utero* refuses to emerge from inside mama until convinced that the world outside the womb is as warm as her present soft berth. A pure delight.

Go and Hush the Baby. By Betsy Byars. Illustrated by Emily McCully, Viking, 1971.

In which an older brother tries to make short shrift of his task—to jolly baby along while mother gets her work done.

Noisy Nora. By Rosemary Wells. Dial, 1974.

Cursed with a demanding baby brother and a know-it-all older sister, poor Nora mouse must learn to gain attention as she can.

Anno's Alphabet: An Adventure in Imagination. By Mitsumasa Anno. Crowell, 1975.

An alphabet book like no other; each wooden letter is both itself and a witty visual surprise.

Dawn. By Uri Shulevitz. Farrar, Straus & Giroux, 1975.

The experience of dawn made miraculously palpable via subtly changing, cameo illustrations and a simple text from the Chinese.

Harry the Fat Bear Spy. By Gahan Wilson. Scribners, 1973.

How Harry, an undercover agent in his native Bearmania, cracks the sticky case of the sabotaged macaroons.

The Devil's Storybook. By Natalie Babbitt. Farrar, Straus & Giroux, 1974.
Ten original, fanciful tales about how old Beelzebub bedevils and is bedeviled by mortals in his worldly wanderings.

What Makes It Go? Work? Fly? Float? By Joe Kaufman. Golden Press, 1972.
In which double-page spreads reveal the innards of ocean liners, transatlantic jets, automobile transmissions and even electric toothbrushes in clear, simplified pictures and text.

Don't Feel Sorry for Paul. By Bernard Wolf. Lippincott, 1974.
A straightforward, moving, but unsentimental photo documentary about a plucky little boy born without properly developed arms or legs and how he manages to manage, with mechanical help.

Index

The names in parentheses following titles of books are those of author and, in italic, illustrator. Italicized page numbers refer to illustrations.

234

Index

Selma G. Lanes

Ever since she memorized both pictures and text of *The Tale
of Corally Crothers* early in a 1930s childhood, Selma G.
Lanes has felt a special affection for young children's books.
For one whole year during World War II she stacked them—
but not before reading all the good ones—at the Fields Corner branch of the Boston Public Library, for thirty-five cents
an hour. She gave them up briefly while earning a B.A. at
Smith College, but eventually wrote a picture book, *Amy
Loves Goodbyes,* and began to review children's books for
the late New York *Herald Tribune*'s *Book Week, Book World*
and *The New York Times Book Review.* She has served as
a consultant to Penguin Books USA on their children's
paperbacks and as a judge (1970) and as director (1972)
of the Children's Spring Book Festival. Mrs. Lanes was one
of three judges for *The New York Times*' Ten Best Illustrated Books of 1973. Since 1974 she has been editor-in-chief of
Parents' Magazine Press. She has two sons and lives in
New York.